GOSPEL ASSURANCE

A 31 DAY GUIDE TO ASSURANCE
MIKE ABENDROTH

A NOCO RADIO MEDIA PRODUCTION

To Marty and Hayley (Abendroth) Horek.

Your desire to honor the Lord Jesus thrills my soul.

PREFACE

I especially want to express my gratitude to Stephen Melniszyn for his friendship and cool artwork, Patty Maciorowski for her all-around help, Paige Fowler for her expertise in formatting this book and John Lawler and Rachel Rathbun for their editing contributions, providing exactly what I needed. The common denominator of all five of these dear saints is their love for Christ-centered preaching and a Christ-dominated ministry.

I am also indebted to my family, especially in this last, trial-filled year. While many people waver during tough times, Kim, Hayley, Marty, Luke, Maddie and Gracie were joyful and walked by faith, not by sight. I am honored to be your husband and father.

PURPOSE

The purpose of this book is simple: it is to give an assurance boost to Christians by directing their attention to Jesus and the doctrine of assurance. For those who already feel secure in Christ, it is designed to ensure that they keep a high level of assurance.

FORMAT

The 31-Day format includes articles written by approximately twenty authors. While you may be familiar with Martin Luther or John Calvin and their writings on assurance, you may be less familiar with other Reformed theologians. I hope to introduce you to some voices on assurance from the last 500 years.

You will find the 31-Day format to be lively and NoCo Radio-like (fast-paced). Also, you will enjoy a variety of formats: this book contains long and short articles, Christ-centered articles, doctrinally-based "Days," some devotional chapters and more. Some "Days" do not directly address assurance as a topic or doctrine, but instead contain truths about Jesus Christ. You might ask, "why does not every 'Day' directly concentrate on assurance?" As you will see as you read the book, it is because assurance and Jesus Christ are tethered together. The more you know about Jesus, the more your assurance will be buoyed.

You will notice that every "Day" has an article followed by five quotes at the end. While the quotes are not necessarily related to the "Day," they are all related to assurance of salvation.

I hope you read it every day for a month, but do not feel the legalistic pressure to do so. Just pick it up when you have time, read the "Day" and then ponder the truths you have learned. You will discover that, as the book progresses, some of the articles require more time and thought. As you grow in your understanding of assurance, the level of instruction will increase. Due to length, a few of the articles split into more than one Day. Do not shy away from longer chapters or chapters that require more thought. The payoff will be worth it. Since habits are established over time, it is my hope, in these thirty-one days, you will begin to establish habits of thinking rightly about Jesus Christ and His salvation.

All of the verses in the book are from the King James Bible. The main reason is that the articles were written by theologians who utilized the KJV. It is a fine translation, and if you are not used to reading Old English, ye soon will be. Trusteth me.

The Appendices contain some wonderful hymns related to the topic of this book and some "Comfortable Words" of the gospel of grace by Thomas Cranmer.

To reiterate, the goal of this book is plain: I want to direct your attention to the Risen Savior, the Lord Jesus, who is your only hope of eternal life and the only sacrifice for sinners like you (and me). And if this book helps your focus on Jesus, assurance is soon to follow.

Only the Preface, Introduction and Appendix 2 are under copyright. The 31 Days are material that falls under public domain.

TABLE OF CONTENTS

Introduction

My goal for the book you hold is simple. I want you to have gospel assurance by fixing your eyes, by faith alone, on Jesus, the Lord of glory.

Martin Luther, known for his direct delivery about faith alone in Jesus Christ alone, also spoke bluntly and reasonably about the assurance of salvation. The German Reformer wrote, "When I look at myself, I do not see how I can be saved. But when I look at Jesus, I do not see how I can be lost." What a wonderful summary of the doctrine of assurance. Pure gospel confidence. "Good news" assurance. Proper thinking about God's secure salvation is essential and invaluable for both a Christian's living and dying. I simply want to emphasize Luther's point that we gain assurance when we focus primarily on the person and work of the Lord Jesus.

As I lay in the hospital bed in the summer of 2021, I contemplated life, death and eternal life. Words like "you have respiratory failure" are not soon forgotten. When you are isolated from family and friends for weeks, there is a lot of time to ponder eternal verities. You hope they are verities. While I was too sick to read and could only listen to the Bible on my phone, I still wanted to think appropriately, even with my oxygen-deprived mind. I still knew I was a sinner and that I had never lived up to the two great laws, "love God" and "love neighbor." If I was going to rely on myself, I understood that the thrice holy God required perfect, entire, exact and perpetual obedience to enter His holy heaven. I grasped the fact that no number of good deeds, civil works or religious deeds could wipe away sins and crimes I committed against the Creator. "The just shall live by faith" resonated with me because my only hope was outside of me. It was Jesus, the One who conquered sin, death and Satan. All that I needed was Jesus' representative life of perfect, entire, exact and perpetual obedience for me and His substitutionary death for my sins. I believed it and continue to believe it. I fell asleep (not the biblical "asleep," signifying death!).

Jesus and Assurance

Jesus and the doctrine of assurance are tethered together. For those struggling with assurance, the vast majority of their spiritual problems could be solved if they diverted their eyes from their trials, troubles, sin and, most problematically, themselves to Jesus. Without Jesus "front and center," doubting, wondering and questioning multiply. The doubting Christian ultimately fears death because they are not confident in what

i

will happen after their last breath on Earth. For them, will it be "gain" when they die?

Much like a compass can get the wanderer back on track, the writer of the Epistle to the Hebrews re-orients struggling Christians. The recipients of the letter were under tremendous persecution and difficulties. I am positive many thought they would lose their lives just like they lost possessions and homes. Again, the possibility of impending death clarifies the mind. It crystalizes one's thoughts. If suffering and persecution can sometimes cause the believer to waver, how much more would the very present reality of death? What did the author say Jesus did? Is Jesus directly linked to assurance? You be the judge:

> *Forasmuch then as the children are partakers of flesh and blood, he also himself likewise took part of the same; that through death he might destroy him that had the power of death, that is, the devil; And deliver them who through fear of death were all their lifetime subject to bondage. For verily he took not on him the nature of angels; but he took on him the seed of Abraham. Wherefore in all things it behooved him to be made like unto his brethren, that he might be a merciful and faithful high priest in things pertaining to God, to make reconciliation for the sins of the people. For in that he himself hath suffered being tempted, he is able to succour them that are tempted. (Hebrews 2:14-18)*

"Succour" is a great word. It means to help, assist, give aid or support. Does that not perfectly describe what the Lord Jesus does? The Son of God gives Christians assistance, especially when they are in difficult and intense predicaments. When you, dear Christian, are at your weakest, you are not without help, but are strengthened by the One who has eternally loved you. Did you know Jesus even renders assistance to those who struggle with their assurance? Why would He help in every other area but not assist with assurance? Jesus is a good shepherd.

Laying prone in the hospital bed, totally helpless (I could only muster up the strength to walk 22 steps a day) and on 60 liters of oxygen a minute, I needed succour. And I needed to know that I could and would receive succour from Jesus Himself. In other words, I needed assurance. I needed assurance that God loved me and that I was His child. Assurance on one's potential deathbed calms the soul. Assurance as one lives also calms the soul. Both the healthy and dying need assurance. Therefore, the more we can learn about the doctrine of assurance, the better. While in the hospital, my friend R. Scott Clark said, "Mike, Jesus loves you. Jesus died for your sins. He was raised for you. You can trust Him. There is no condemnation for those in Christ Jesus." Succour, indeed, even through another Christian.

A DOUBLE FOCUS

There is a potential risk in publishing a book on the assurance of salvation. The Baptist preacher Charles Spurgeon reportedly stated something akin to, "If you chase the dove of assurance of salvation, you never seem to catch it. But if you pursue, by faith alone, the Lord Jesus Christ, the dove of assurance gently comes and settles upon your shoulders." What a travesty it would be if the very book meant to help Christians ended up hurting them. The good news is that this "31-Day Guide" book does not simply focus upon the believer's confidence and certainty of their salvation. While it accomplishes that, it also directs the reader's attention to grace incarnate, the risen Lord and Savior, Jesus of Nazareth. In other words, if you walk by faith in the Son of God and fix your eyes upon Him, you should regularly expect to have the settled assurance that is so sweet to every Christian. This is the very purpose of the following compilation of essays and "ancient" articles: that every saint would enjoy their assurance just as a son or daughter enjoys knowing that they are their father's child – no matter what occurs.

QUESTIONS

Allow me to ask you some direct questions:

- ♦ Do you have assurance of your salvation?
- ♦ When you die, will God accept you into His holy Heaven?
- ♦ Do you believe you will survive Judgment Day?
- ♦ Despite your daily struggle to live righteously and war against sin, do you have a settled confidence that you are a child of God?
- ♦ Is every one of your sins forgiven? How do you know?
- ♦ Are you completely cleansed by the blood of the Lamb?
- ♦ Have you been accepted by God the Father through Christ the Son by the Holy Spirit?
- ♦ Are you sure it is possible to know if you are really saved and secure from the torments of Hell?
- ♦ Can you say with a bold confidence, "The Son of God loved me and gave himself for me"? (Galatians 2:20)
- ♦ Is it presumptuous to have assurance?
- ♦ Some religions teach that assurance is sinful. Are they right?

Thankfully, the Bible contains all the help every Christian needs to sort through the doctrine of assurance. Scripture is sufficient. What is even more wonderful? The triune God wants every Christian, He wants you, believer, to know that you are His child. The Apostle John famously penned, "These things have I written unto you that believe on the name of the Son of God; that ye may know that ye have eternal life, and that ye may believe on the name of the Son of God" (1 John 5:13). From this concept and 2 Timothy 1:12 ("for I know whom I have believed, and am persuaded that he is able to keep that which I have committed unto him against that day,") Major Daniel Whittle famously wrote the hymn "I Know Whom I Have Believed." Can you sing it from the bottom of your soul? Do you wish you could sing it? Or even hum along with heartfelt agreement?

> *I know not why God's wondrous grace*
> *To me He hath made known,*
> *Nor why, unworthy, Christ in love*
> *Redeemed me for His own.*

> Refrain:
> *But "I know Whom I have believed,*
> *And am persuaded that He is able*
> *To keep that which I've committed*
> *Unto Him against that day."*

THE PRIMARY FOCUS

Most evangelicals struggling with their assurance start their search in the wrong place. While there is a time for looking to oneself (more on this later), this cannot be the primary place you set your attention. Instead, you should look to Jesus Christ by faith. The author of the Epistle to the Hebrews writes, "Looking unto Jesus the author and finisher of our faith; who for the joy that was set before him endured the cross, despising the shame, and is set down at the right hand of the throne of God" (Hebrews 12:2). He is precisely the One whom we must concentrate on and to whom we must look. To use the language of the theologians, gaze, by faith, to "Christ for you" (Christ for pardon). To what degree is He "for us?" A cursory review of the first eleven chapters of Hebrews will amply supply the answer. Jesus is your Prophet and King, but in Hebrews, the emphasis is on His role as Priest. He has not only earned the righteousness which the Father justly required, but He, Jesus, paid for all our unrighteousness as the sacrifice. The Risen Savior is "for you!" He is such a great high priest that the only right response is "trust!"

> *Seeing then that we have a great high priest, that is passed into the heavens, Jesus the Son of God, let us hold fast our profession. For we have not an high priest which cannot be touched with the feeling of our infirmities; but was in all points tempted like as we are, yet without sin. Let us therefore come boldly unto the throne of grace, that we may obtain mercy, and find grace to help in time of need. (Hebrews 4:14-16)*

The author's focus on the Lord Jesus reminds Christians of the perfect and objective work of Christ. Believers are directed, by the Holy Spirit, to consider the person of Jesus and to meditate upon Him. Is that where you look? Evie Nichols, my grandmother-in-law, often quipped, "When you gaze upon the Lord Jesus and only glance at your problems, all is well. But when you reverse that order, bad things happen." Wise counsel. If you only "glance at the Lord Jesus and gaze on your problems," then watch out. Now let me change Grandma Evie's slogan a bit, or at least narrow her focus: "Make sure you gaze upon the Lord Jesus and only glance at yourself, or your assurance of salvation will abandon you." Indeed, focusing on Jesus is fundamental to living in joy, peace and freedom. But if you only glance at Jesus as you gaze inwards, you will constantly be trying to deal with your sins to feel right with God. The more this happens, the more "trust" is replaced with "effort." You will be sin-focused instead of Christ-focused. It will leave you uncertain, unassured and exhausted. Assurance, exit stage left.

THE SECONDARY FOCUS

Rather than keeping Christ as the primary focus, the default "look" for most believers places Him in a secondary role as "Christ in you" (Christ for power). While "Christ for you" moves the attention outside the believer, "Christ in you" recognizes the work of the Holy Spirit in the believer, which happens because of the believer's union with Jesus Christ. It is internal and categorized as "subjective" because it is not humanly measurable. Christ for pardon is in the category of justification, and Christ for power is in sanctification's category. We rejoice that both are true, yet we want to make sure we never make our holy living the ground for our salvation. The only ground must be perfect and "Christ for you" is, in fact, perfect.

Charles Hodge, in his popular three-volume *Systematic Theology*, issues a proper warning:

v

Many sincere believers are too introspective. They look too exclusively within, so that their hope is graduated [grows] by the degree of evidence of regeneration which they find in their own experience. This, except in rare cases, can never lead to the assurance of hope. We may examine our hearts with all the microscopic care prescribed by President Edwards in his work on "The Religious Affections," and never be satisfied that we have eliminated every ground of misgiving and doubt.

If you do not look first to the Lord Jesus, you will easily veer off to one of these two options. You will either think self-righteously (that you somehow believe you keep God's law or lessen it to make it possible to obey) or you will become full of despair (realizing how far you fall from keeping God's holy law). The self-righteous deceive themselves by thinking that they are actually living up to the law of God (for their standing), while those more honest with themselves despair that they are not measuring up to God's standards. Indeed, focusing on oneself while only glancing at Jesus is a schizophrenic focal point that can lead to frustration and uncertainty. For instance, you were probably taught that after you come to Christ in faith, you will look more and more like the Lord Jesus and be very convicted when you sin (true!). At the same time, you may also have been taught that as you grow in faith, you will become more and more aware of the sin in your life. So as you grow, you both desire to sin less and realize that you sin more. This inward analysis will cause you to echo the beginning of Luther's famous line we read earlier: "When I look at myself, I do not see how I can be saved." It is a hamster wheel of doubt. But when we balance that inward glance by focusing primarily on the finished work of the Lord Jesus, it provides the antidote.

What about fruit? Is not fruit important? Do I have the "root" (Christ) if I do not have much "fruit" (evidence)? Focusing on Jesus, the only standing of one's salvation, will inevitably lead to fruit and evidence in the life of the Christian. As the old adage goes, "We are saved by faith alone, but that faith will not be alone." A Christian's faith works. But don't measure your acceptance in God's sight by anything less than perfection, that is, Jesus, the perfect One who always pleased the Father. While justification and sanctification are similar in that they both are divine graces and both occur the instant a person is saved, they differ in that justification is a one-time declaration and sanctification is progressive. You cannot have one without the other, but they are not the same. Justification is Christ for pardon (declared righteous) and sanctification is Christ for power (to kill sin and live unto righteousness).

Read these John Calvin quotes from his *Institutes of the Christian Religion* and rest in God's work for you, keeping your spiritual eyesight centered on the right object and away from yourself:

> *If they [believers] begin to judge their salvation by good works, nothing will be more uncertain or more feeble; for indeed, if works be judged of themselves, by their imperfection they will no less declare God's wrath than by their incomplete purity they testify to his benevolence (3.14.19).*

> *For nothing so moves us to repose our assurance and certainty of mind in the Lord as distrust of ourselves, and the anxiety occasioned by the awareness of our ruin (3.2.23).*

> *For faith totters if it pays attention to works, since no one, even of the most holy, will find there anything on which to rely (3.11.11).*

If you interrogate yourself with questions like, "Do I love God?" or "Do I love my neighbor?" you had better soften the questions so that they sound more like this: "Do I want to love God?" "Am I sorry when I do not love God?" "Do I wish I loved God more?" The desire of every Christian is to love God, but Christians fall short. Yes, even Christians sin. Christians repent. Since this section is all about asking questions, how about this one: "Who gave you the desire to love God?" The answer is the Holy Spirit Himself, which demonstrates that you are a Christian.

The common denominator in the questions posed in the last paragraph is that they are all law questions. Law requires doing. It requires action. Your action. Your obedience. There is nothing wrong with God's law because it is holy and good, but the law should force you to keep searching. In other words, it should spur you on to look for some good news for law breakers, i.e., the Gospel. The Gospel is what the triune God has done for law breakers. It is all God's doing. It is completely God's action. Which one would offer the best assurance, your law keeping or God's saving work in His Son? Neither the law nor your obedience offers a ground of assurance. Should we love Jesus? Yes. Must we obey Jesus? Yes! Will we, by the indwelling power of the Holy Spirit, love Jesus more and more? Of course, but Christians need to rest in the Son of God who perfectly fulfilled the law for us.

For the Christian who does not love the Lord with all their heart, soul, mind and strength (Matthew 22:37-40), there is hope in the Lord Jesus, who on Earth, perfectly and exactly loved His Lord with all His heart, soul, mind and strength! Jesus did not have to obey for Himself because

He was already inherently righteous. He obeyed for us. He kept the law for you, Christian. Jesus earned complete righteousness for every Christian. That is good news and that is an objective truth. Do you see it by faith? Do you not want to respond with gratitude and seek to obey God's law which guides Christians?

Ready for some more conviction?

- How was your "Quiet Time" today?
- Did you read your Bible enough today?
- When was the last time you preached the Gospel to anyone?
- Have you been self-sacrificial in your love for others, your spouse, your children? And now for the most convicting question (for most, including me):
- How is your prayer life? Last month? Last week? Today? (ouch!)

All these "law" questions are appropriate in their place, but their place is never first place, and they should never be the "ground of salvation." John Calvin is again instructive, writing:

> *The consciences of believers, in seeking assurance of their justification before God, should rise above and advance beyond the law, forgetting all law righteousness...For there the question is not how we may become righteous but how, being unrighteous and unworthy, we may be reckoned righteous. If consciences wish to attain any certainty in this matter, they ought to give no place to the law. Nor can anyone rightly infer from this that the law is superfluous for believers, since it does not stop teaching and exhorting and urging them to good, even though before God's judgment seat it has no place in their consciences (Institutes, 3.19.2).*

ENCOURAGEMENT

Ready for some more encouragement?

- Jesus read and studied the Old Testament enough
- Jesus preached the Gospel enough
- Jesus' sacrifice for His family, friends and enemies was enough
- Jesus prayed enough. His prayer life was perfect
- Jesus said "It is finished."
- Jesus is enough and did enough (remember Jesus obeyed for others, not Himself)

◆ Jesus' resurrection demonstrated God was fully satisfied and that Jesus was who he claimed to be

I am not saying that there is never a time to look to self to see the fruit of the Spirit of God in you. However, I am saying that you should never start and end with looking only unto yourself. Sinclair Ferguson warned, "So long as there is a vestige of reliance upon our righteousness, our service, our obedience, our knowledge, our understanding of doctrine, there can be no genuine assurance."

What Horatius Bonar wrote in his book *God's Way of Holiness* perfectly applies to the assurance of salvation. He said,

> *The secret of a believer's holy walk is his continual recurrence to the blood of the Surety, and his daily [communion] with a crucified and risen Lord. All divine life, and all precious fruits of it, pardon, peace, and holiness, spring from the cross. All fancied sanctification which does not arise wholly from the blood of the cross is nothing better than Pharisaism. If we would be holy, we must get to the cross, and dwell there; else, notwithstanding all our labor, diligence, fasting, praying, and good works, we shall be yet void of real sanctification, destitute of those humble, gracious tempers which accompany a clear view of the cross.*

BOTH ARE TRUE

Can you spot both the objective (Christ for you) and subjective (Christ in you) in 2 Peter 1:1-11?

> *Simon Peter, a servant and an apostle of Jesus Christ, to them that have obtained like precious faith with us through the righteousness of God and our Saviour Jesus Christ: Grace and peace be multiplied unto you through the knowledge of God, and of Jesus our Lord, According as his divine power hath given unto us all things that pertain unto life and godliness, through the knowledge of him that hath called us to glory and virtue: Whereby are given unto us exceeding great and precious promises: that by these ye might be partakers of the divine nature, having escaped the corruption that is in the world through lust.*
>
> *And beside this, giving all diligence, add to your faith virtue; and to virtue knowledge; And to knowledge temperance; and to temperance patience; and to patience godliness; And to godliness brotherly kindness; and to brotherly kindness charity. For if these things be in you, and abound, they make you that ye shall neither be barren nor unfruitful in the knowledge of our Lord*

Jesus Christ. But he that lacketh these things is blind, and cannot see afar off, and hath forgotten that he was purged from his old sins. Wherefore the rather, brethren, give diligence to make your calling and election sure: for if ye do these things, ye shall never fall: For so an entrance shall be ministered unto you abundantly into the everlasting kingdom of our Lord and Saviour Jesus Christ.

I purposely put a space/break in the section, right between verse four and verse five, so that you could observe what Peter is saying with greater ease. The bottom line: follow Robert Murray M'Cheyne's advice and look to the Lord Jesus ten times the amount you look to yourself. Preach to yourself, "Christ for pardon" (Christ for you) and "Christ for power" (Christ in you).

Another approach is set forth in a "True/False" statement:

- True or False: "the just shall live by faith"?
- True or False: "the just shall live by faithfulness"?

The first one is shorthand for "the just shall live by faith in the Lord Jesus Christ, the risen Savior." The second one is not shorthand; it declares, "just people are faithful." Now, do you see the difference? If I were to ask you, "How do you know you are a Christian?", most responses, including yours, will probably be, "I am baptized, I am a member of a church, I pray, I serve, I evangelize and I…" I rejoice you do those things, but make certain you understand the difference between faith (in the object of the risen Lord Jesus) and faithfulness (our obedience). What you do does not make you a Christian. It does not make you a person of faith. In his letter to the Ephesians, Paul was very clear to first teach that we are "in Christ" (chapters 1-3) before telling us how to live for Christ (chapters 4-6). Thus, the answer to the question of "how do you know you are a Christian" should be, "Because I trust in the person and work of Jesus, who lived for me, died for me and was raised for me." You could add, "God even gave me my faith to trust Him. I believe because of grace alone."

CONCLUSION

Dear Christian, remember that nothing in us is perfect, so your assurance can never be perfect. Thomas Brooks concurs, "Our knowledge of God, of Christ, of ourselves, and of the blessed Scripture… is imperfect in this life. And how then can our assurance be perfect?" Therefore, keep walking by faith alone, in Jesus Christ alone, by grace alone.

Rehearse and memorize these verses:

And we know that the Son of God is come, and hath given us an understanding, that we may know him that is true, and we are in him that is true, even in his Son Jesus Christ. This is the true God, and eternal life. (1 John 5:20)

There is therefore now no condemnation to them which are in Christ Jesus. (Romans 8:1)

All that the Father giveth me shall come to me; and him that cometh to me I will in no wise cast out. (John 6:37)

The thief cometh not, but for to steal, and to kill, and to destroy: I am come that they might have life, and that they might have it more abundantly. (John 10:10)

My sheep hear my voice, and I know them, and they follow me: And I give unto them eternal life; and they shall never perish, neither shall any man pluck them out of my hand. My Father, which gave them me, is greater than all; and no man is able to pluck them out of my Father's hand. I and my Father are one. (John 10:27-30)

Are not those verses wonderful and Christ-centered? Speaking of wonderful and Christ-centered, missionary Adoniram Judson said to Madison University students,

Brethren, look to Jesus. This sight will fill you with the greatest consolation and delight. Look to Him on the cross; so great is His love, that, if He had a 1000 lives, He would lay them all down for your redemption. Look to Him on the throne; His blessed countenance fills all heaven with delight and felicity. Look to Him in affliction; He will succor you. Look to Him in death; He will sustain you. Look to Him in judgment; He will save you.

PSALM 130

Did you know that even the venerable English Puritan (my favorite) John Owen had issues with his own assurance? He said, "I myself preached Christ some years when I had but very little, if any, experimental acquaintance with access to God through Christ." Preaching Christ is one thing, but being certain of one's salvation is another. Owen experienced "horror and darkness," but then began mediating on a Psalm. I direct your attention to the same Psalm, and I trust that it will do the same for you as it did for John Owen. And, if you are not stressed about your assurance because you are in a wonderful season of full assurance, you still need this Psalm so you can keep that precious gift of the certainty of your salvation.

Owen said, "God graciously relieved my spirit by a powerful application" upon the study of Psalm 130, a Psalm that plumbs the depths of a soul's anguish to what Spurgeon called, "the heights of assurance."

PSALM 130: SONG OF DEGREES

Out of the depths have I cried unto thee, O LORD.

Lord, hear my voice: let thine ears be attentive to the voice of my supplications.

If thou, LORD, shouldest mark iniquities, O Lord, who shall stand?

But there is forgiveness with thee, that thou mayest be feared. I wait for the LORD, my soul doth wait, and in his word do I hope.

My soul waiteth for the Lord more than they that watch for the morning: I say, more than they that watch for the morning.

Let Israel hope in the LORD: for with the LORD there is mercy, and with him is plenteous redemption.

And he shall redeem Israel from all his iniquities.

Please reread Psalm 130 right now. Is it not good to rest in God's mercy? How delightful it is to take the triune God at His word and believe His promises of forgiveness and redemption? Jesus is alive. Jesus loves Christians. Believer, Jesus loves you. You can trust Him for everything, including your eternal soul.

Owen went on to comment, "Faith's discovery of forgiveness in God is the great supportment of a sin-perplexed soul." While I have never seen the word "supportment," I think I understand its meaning. And so do you. Is not the Lord good? Does not the Lord do good, especially to you? The exact truth Owen taught and believed is found in the works of another trustworthy Puritan author, Thomas Brooks, who echoed Owen:

Now, when any fears, or darkness, or doubts, or disputes arise in your souls about your spiritual state, oh, then, run to Christ in the promise, and plead the promise, and let your souls cleave close to the promise: for this is the way of ways to have your evidences cleared, your comforts restored, your peace maintained, your graces strengthened, and your assurance raised and confirmed.

May this book direct your attention to the center of the universe, the Lord Jesus. If you want assurance of your salvation, Jesus is the key. If you desire a sure confidence that your sins are forgiven, the Son of Man must be central. The assurance of salvation is never to be divorced from the King of kings, Christ Jesus. What is true for Christian growth is true for Christian assurance. Sinclair Ferguson agrees,

The ability to focus our gaze, fill our minds, and devote our hearts to Jesus Christ is a basic element in real Christian growth. Inability to do so is a sign of immaturity... Some Christians never appear to make much spiritual progress. Spiritual focus and concentration are beyond them. They seem to be dominated by feelings, rather than the gospel. Their powers of concentration on spiritual realities are underdeveloped. They find it difficult to devote their attention to Christ in private or in public, in prayer, in singing God's praise, or in reading His word.

Now let's start your journey! Day One awaits.

Mike Abendroth
June 2022

DAY 1

THE PERSON AND WORK OF CHRIST
BY JAMES SMITH

(James Smith was a predecessor of Charles Spurgeon at New Park Street
Chapel in London from 1841 until 1850.)

WHAT A WONDERFUL PERSON is my glorious Lord Jesus! All the
divine attributes are found in Him. As there are no limits to His fullness -
there can be no limit to my supplies, or the least prospect of need. Jesus
is my divine Savior!

His *bounty* will supply me,
His *omnipotence* will deliver me,
His *omnipresence* will protect me,
His *omniscience* will guard me,
His *love* will animate me,
His *mercy* will heal me,
His *grace* will support me,
His *compassion* will comfort me,
His *pity* will relieve me,
His *goodness* will provide for me,
His *tenderness* will soothe me,
His *kindness* will encourage me,
His *patience* will bear with me,
His *justice* will avenge me,
His *faithfulness* will embolden me,
His *holiness* will beautify me,
His *anger* will awe me,
His *life* will quicken me,
His *light* will illumine me,
His *Word* will regulate me,
His *joy* will delight me,
His *blessedness* will elevate me,
His *long-suffering* will lead me to repentance,
His *immutability* will secure the fulfillment of all the promises to me,
His *truth* will be my shield and buckler,
His *sovereignty* will raise my admiration,
His *condescension* will inspire me with gratitude and love,
and His *all-sufficiency* will satisfy me both in time and eternity!

In Jesus, God has reconciled me to Himself, imputing my trespasses to
Him, and His obedience to me.

God by Jesus, takes away all my sins, His own wrath, and my deserved condemnation! All good things are treasured up in Christ, were procured for me by Christ, flow to me through Christ, and are conferred on me for the sake of Christ!

How exactly suited is the Lord Jesus to my case! Inflexible justice demands my blood - but He becomes my substitute, and spills His own! In Jesus, I see my sin and God's justice meet! He removes the one and satisfies the other!

WHAT IS JESUS CALLED IN GOD'S HOLY WORD?

- ♦ **A Savior** - in reference to my lost condition
- ♦ **A Reconciler** - in reference to the enmity that existed between myself and God
- ♦ **A Redeemer** - in reference to my slavery to sin
- ♦ **A Mediator** - in respect to the disagreement between myself and the Most High God
- ♦ **A Refiner** - with respect to my filthiness
- ♦ **An Advocate** - with regard to my perplexed cause
- ♦ **A Prophet** - in respect to my ignorance
- ♦ **A Priest** - with a view to my guiltiness
- ♦ **A King** - in regard to my weakness and foes
- ♦ **A Bridegroom** - regarding my lowly estate and relationship
- ♦ **A Physician** - with regard to my many soul maladies

In a word, Jesus is "All In All."

Oh to know more of Jesus in
The glory of His person,
The riches of His grace,
The perfection of His work,
The tenderness of His heart,
The strength of His love and
The effectual working of His power!

If one dear saint of God had perished, so might all; if one of the covenant ones be lost, so may all be; and then there is no gospel promise true, but the Bible is a lie, and there is nothing in it worth my acceptance.

I will be an infidel at once when I can believe that a saint of God can ever fall finally. If God hath loved me once, then He will love me forever.
- C.H. Spurgeon

Our reconciliation to God is permanent and eternal. Because Christ accomplished it for us, there is no possibility it can ever be undone. Though we continue, even as believers, to do those things that in themselves deserve God's displeasure, we can never revert to a state of divine alienation. For the sake of Christ, God will always accept us. And even when God deems it necessary to discipline us for persistent disobedience, He always does so out of love to restore us to the way of obedience (see Hebrews 12:4-11). *- Jerry Bridges*

If the elect could perish then Jesus Christ should be very unfaithful to His Father because God the Father hath given this charge to Christ, that whomsoever He elected, Christ should preserve them safe, to bring them to heaven (John 6:39). *- Christopher Love*

[Our Lord] is ready to receive all who [come] to Him, however unworthy they may feel themselves. None who repent and believe are too bad to be enrolled in the ranks of Christ's army. All who come to Him by faith are admitted, clothed, armed, trained, and finally led on to complete victory. Fear not to begin this very day. There is yet room for you. *- J.C. Ryle*

I am wholly His; I am peculiarly His; I am universally His; I am eternally His. *- Thomas Brooks*

DAY 2

HE CARES FOR ME!
BY CHARLES SPURGEON

Casting all your care upon Him for He cares for you! - 1 Peter 5:7

IT IS A HAPPY WAY of soothing sorrow, when we can feel "He cares for me!" Christian! Do not dishonor God, by always wearing a brow of worry! Come, cast your burden upon your God! You are staggering beneath a weight which your Father would not feel.

What seems like a crushing burden to you would be but as small dust to Him.

Nothing is so sweet as to, "Lie passive in God's hands, and know no will, but His." O child of suffering - be patient! God has not overlooked you in His providence. He who is the feeder of sparrows will also furnish you with what you need. Do not sit down in despair.

THERE IS ONE WHO CARES FOR YOU:

- **His all-seeing eye** is fixed on you!
- **His all-loving heart** beats with pity for your woe!
- **His omnipotent hand** shall yet bring you the needed help!
- **The darkest cloud** shall scatter itself in showers of mercy.
- **The blackest gloom** shall give place to the morning light.

If you are one of His family, He will bind up your wounds, and heal your broken heart. Do not doubt His grace, because of your troubles, but believe that He loves you as much in seasons of distress as in times of happiness. What a serene and quiet life might you lead, if you would leave providing to the God of providence!

If God cares for you, why need you care also? Can you trust Him for your soul and not for your body? He has never refused to bear your burdens. He has never fainted under their weight. Come, then, soul! Be done with fretful worry and leave all your concerns in the hand of your gracious God!

If the faith whereby I have laid hold on Christ to be my Savior be altogether wrought in me by the Holy Ghost through grace, then I defy the devil to take away that which he never gave me or to crush that which Jehovah Himself created in me. I defy my free will to fling what it never brought to me. What God has given, created, introduced, and established in the heart; He will maintain there. - *C.H. Spurgeon*

If Christ has once possessed the affections, there is no dispossessing of him again. A fire in the heart overcomes all fires without. - *Richard Sibbes*

The assurance of His total forgiveness of our sins through the blood of Christ means we don't have to play defensive games anymore. We don't have to rationalize and excuse our sins. We can call sin exactly what it is, regardless of how ugly and shameful it may be, because we know that Jesus bore that sin in His body on the cross. - *Jerry Bridges*

Your Rock is Christ, and it is not the Rock which ebbs and flows, but your sea. - *Samuel Rutherford*

Let us not seek any other ground of assurance than God's own testimony. - *John Calvin*

DAY 3

THE INFINITE OCEAN OF CHRIST'S LOVE!
BY OCTAVIUS WINSLOW

THE MIND HAS OFTEN been sensible of a feeling of awe as we have stood upon the shore, and gazed upon the vast expanse of the ocean. With a similar, yet far transcending emotion, we approach the infinite ocean of Christ's love!

Like the eternity of God, we cannot fathom where His love begins, or where it terminates. There is no other solution to the marvelous mysteries of His Incarnation and Sacrificial Death but this: Christ has loved us. Love originated all, explains all, illustrates all. Love is the interpreter of every Divine mystery.

There is not a circumstance of our Lord's history which is not another form or manifestation of love:

- **His incarnation** is love stooping
- **His sympathy** is love weeping
- **His compassion** is love supporting
- **His grace** is love acting
- **His teaching** is the voice of love
- **His silence** is the repose of love
- **His patience** is the restraint of love
- **His obedience** is the labor of love
- **His suffering** is the travail of love
- **His cross** is the altar of love
- **His death** is the burnt offering of love
- **His resurrection** is the triumph of love
- **His ascension** into heaven is the enthronement of love
- **His sitting down** at the right hand of God is the intercession of love

Such is the deep, the vast, the boundless ocean of Christ's love! The soul muses in silent awe as it gazes upon this fathomless, limitless sea! Nothing short of a divine love could or would have borne our sins, and the punishment of our sins. The weight of the one, and the terribleness of the other, would have crushed and annihilated a mere 'created' affection. There existed no love but the love of Jesus equal to the work of salvation.

Who was willing, who was able, to bear that heavy load, to endure that overwhelming curse, but Jesus? Oh, think, beloved reader, what the love of Christ has done and suffered for you...

The burden it bore, the sorrow it felt, the humiliation it underwent, the insults, the ignominy, the privation through which it traveled; its groans, its sighs, its tears, its darkness, how inconceivably it agonized, how freely it bled, how voluntarily it died, the sins it has pardoned, the guilt it has cleansed, the declensions it has restored, the backslidings it has healed, the sorrows it has soothed, the patience it has exercised, the gentleness it has exhibited, and then ask, could any other but the love of Jesus have done all this, and endured all this? Such is the love of Christ!

To have saved us upon such terms: a stoop so low, a humiliation so profound, a labor so immense, mental anguish so acute, bodily suffering so agonizing, a death so ignominious. Was ever love like this? Was it ever equaled? Where shall we find its parallel? Love less divine, less strong, less gentle, could never have won your heart, uprooted your enmity, tore you from your idols; enthroning Christ, all of Christ, Christ only, Christ supremely, Christ forever! The love of Christ will be the wonder, the study, and the song of all pure, holy intelligences through eternity!

Beloved, *nothing* shall take the love of Christ from you, or separate you from it. It does not ebb with the ebbing of your feelings; it does not chill with the chill of your affections; it does not change with the changing scenes and circumstances of your life. The love of Christ has depths we cannot sound, heights we cannot explore, an infinite fulness and freeness tiding over all the sins, infirmities, and sorrows of its blessed and favored objects.

Seek to know this love of Christ, though it is so vast that it "passes knowledge." Infinite though it is, you may experience its reality, taste its sweetness, and be influenced by its all commanding, all constraining power. Do not limit your heart experience of Christ's love, for it is infinite in its nature, and boundless in its extent.

As yet, how many of us stand but upon the shore of this ocean! How little do we know, experimentally, of the love of Christ in our souls! Bring your heart with its profoundest emptiness, its most startling discovery of sin, its lowest frame, its deepest sorrow, and sink it into the depths of the Savior's love! That infinite sea will flow over all, erase all, absorb all, and your soul shall swim and sport amid its gentle waves, exclaiming in your joy and transport, "Oh, the depths!"

The Lord direct your heart into the love of God! Just as it is: hard, cold, fickle, sinful, sad and sorrowful.

- Christ's love touching your hard heart, will dissolve it
- Christ's love touching your cold heart, will warm it
- Christ's love touching your sinful heart, will purify it
- Christ's love touching your sorrowful heart, will soothe it
- Christ's love touching your wandering heart, will draw it back to Himself

Only bring your heart to Christ's love!

Believe that He loves you, and just as love begets love, so the simple belief in the love of Jesus will inspire you with a reflected, responsive affection; and your soul, like the flower, will burst from its captivity, and bloom, and, soaring in life, liberty, and beauty, will float in the sunbeams of Gods full, free, and eternal love; and, in a little while, will find itself in heaven, where all is love!

"Blessed Jesus! Your love, like Your agonies, is an unknown and unfathomable depth! It passes knowledge. Let it rise and expand before me, until it fills the entire scope of my soul's vision; occupies every niche of my heart; and bears me onward by its all commanding, all constraining influence, in the path of a holy loving obedience and surrender."

May you experience the love of Christ, though it is so great you will never fully understand it. - Ephesians 3:19

Faith alone justifies, through Christ alone. Assurance is the enjoyment of that justification. - *Sinclair Ferguson*

The assurance that we are called of God, chosen in Christ before the foundation of the world, affords a safe and secure anchorage from which no tempest can ever dislodge us. - *James Philip*

Christ is to be answerable for all those that are given to Him, at the last day, and therefore we need not doubt but that He will certainly employ all the power of His Godhead to secure and save all those that He must be accountable for. Christ's charge and care of these that are given to Him, extends even to the very day of their resurrection, that He may not so much as lose their dust, but gather it together again, and raise it up in glory to be a proof of His fidelity; for, saith He, "I shall lose nothing, but raise it up again at the last day." - *Thomas Brooks*

No less a person than God is needed to assure us of God's love.
- *Richard Sibbes*

Upon what ground is this certainty built? Surely not upon anything that is in us. Our assurance of perseverance is grounded wholly upon God. If we look upon ourselves, we see cause of fear and doubting; but if we look up to God, we shall find cause enough for assurance.
- *Arthur Hildersham*

DAY 4

CHRISTIAN PROGRESS
BY JOHN ANGELL JAMES

He will feed His flock like a shepherd. He will carry the lambs in His arms, holding them close to His heart. - Isaiah 40:11

DWELL UPON THE LOVE and tenderness of our Lord Jesus! Notice who are the objects of His care - "the lambs," which means not only those of tender age but also those who have been newly converted; those who are young in Christian experience; and also those whose temperament is naturally timid, whose strength is feeble, and whose danger is great.

Yes, you are the objects of Christ's special attention, care, and solicitude! You are those whom He takes up in the arms of His power and lays on the bosom of His love! He knows… your weakness, your timidity, your dangers! He will exert for you His tenderest sympathy, His greatest vigilance, His mightiest power.

This expression however not only conveys the idea of great care of the weak but the exercise of that care with a view to their preservation and growth. It means not only that He cordially receives them, will provide for their safety, be concerned for their comfort, and will accommodate His conduct to their needs but He will also nourish them through their infant existence, and raise them up to maturity and strength. Let every lamb of the flock of Christ, therefore, go to Him by faith and prayer, and say...

"Blessed Jesus, I come to you as a poor, weak, and trembling creature, doubtful of my own continuance, and alarmed at my numerous difficulties and enemies. I am but a lamb, and often fear I shall never be anything better. But was it not in regard to such weakness that You have been pleased to utter these gracious and tender words? I flee to you as the helpless lamb to its shepherd: when hungry, to feed it or when pursued by wild beasts, that he may defend it. Lord, take me in the arms of Your power and lay me on the bosom of Your love, though I am so poor and helpless a creature. I will hope in your nurturing power and love, that I shall continue to grow, and that You will one day rejoice in me, as one of the flock which You have purchased with Your own blood!"

Never did a believer in Jesus Christ die or drown in his voyage to heaven. They will all be found safe and sound with the Lamb on mount Zion. Christ loseth none of them; yea, nothing of them. (John vi. 39.) Not a bone of a believer is to be seen in the field of battle. They are all more than conquerors through Him that loved them." (Rom. viii. 37.)
- *Robert Traill*

Uncertainty as to our relationship with God is one of the most enfeebling and dispiriting of things. It makes a man heartless. It takes the pith out of him. He cannot fight; he cannot run. He is easily dismayed and gives way. He can do nothing for God. But when we know that we are of God, we are vigorous, brave, invincible. There is no more quickening truth than this of assurance. - *Horatius Bonar*

To be assured of our salvation is no arrogant stoutness. It is faith. It is devotion. It is not presumption. It is God's promise. - *Augustine*

Assurance will be a golden shield to beat back temptation, and will triumph over it. - *Thomas Watson*

And though the assurance of sense be the sweetest, yet the assurance of faith is the surest assurance; for what you get in hand from God you may soon lose the benefit and comfort of it; but what you have upon bond in the promise, is still secure. - *Ralph Erskine*

DAY 5

THE CANONS OF DORT (1618-1619)
The Fifth Main Point of Doctrine - The Perseverance of the Saints

ARTICLE 8: The Certainty of this Preservation
So it is not by their own merits or strength but by God's undeserved mercy that they neither forfeit faith and grace totally nor remain in their downfalls to the end and are lost. With respect to themselves this not only easily could happen, but also undoubtedly would happen; but with respect to God it cannot possibly happen. God's plan cannot be changed; God's promise cannot fail; the calling according to God's purpose cannot be revoked; the merit of Christ as well as his interceding and preserving cannot be nullified; and the sealing of the Holy Spirit can neither be invalidated nor wiped out.

ARTICLE 9: The Assurance of this Preservation
Concerning this preservation of those chosen to salvation and concerning the perseverance of true believers in faith, believers themselves can and do become assured in accordance with the measure of their faith. By this faith they firmly believe that they are and always will remain true and living members of the church, and that they have the forgiveness of sins and eternal life.

ARTICLE 10: The Ground of this Assurance
Accordingly, this assurance does not derive from some private revelation beyond or outside the Word, but from faith in the promises of God which are very plentifully revealed in the Word for our comfort, from the testimony of "the Holy Spirit testifying with our spirit that we are God's children and heirs" (Rom. 8:16-17), and finally from a serious and holy pursuit of a clear conscience and of good works. If God's chosen ones in this world did not have this well-founded comfort that the victory will be theirs and this reliable guarantee of eternal glory, they would be of all people most miserable.

ARTICLE 11: Doubts Concerning this Assurance
Meanwhile, Scripture testifies that believers have to contend in this life with various doubts of the flesh, and that under severe temptation they do not always experience this full assurance of faith and certainty of perseverance. But God, the Father of all comfort, "does not let them be tempted beyond what they can bear, but with the temptation he also provides a way out" (1 Cor. 10:13), and by the Holy Spirit revives in them the assurance of their perseverance.

ARTICLE 12: This Assurance as an Incentive to Godliness

This assurance of perseverance, however, so far from making true believers proud and carnally self-assured, is rather the true root of humility, of childlike respect, of genuine godliness, of endurance in every conflict, of fervent prayers, of steadfastness in cross bearing and in confessing the truth, and of well-founded joy in God. Reflecting on this benefit provides an incentive to a serious and continual practice of thanksgiving and good works, as is evident from the testimonies of Scripture and the examples of the saints.

ARTICLE 13: Assurance No Inducement to Carelessness

Neither does the renewed confidence of perseverance produce immorality or lack of concern for godliness in those put back on their feet after a fall, but it produces a much greater concern to observe carefully the ways which the Lord prepared in advance. They observe these ways in order that by walking in them they may maintain the assurance of their perseverance, lest, by their abuse of God's fatherly goodness, the face of the gracious God (for the godly, looking upon that face is sweeter than life, but its withdrawal is more bitter than death) turn away from them again, with the result that they fall into greater anguish of spirit.

ARTICLE 14: God's Use of Means in Perseverance

And, just as it has pleased God to begin this work of grace in us by the proclamation of the gospel, so God preserves, continues, and completes this work by the hearing and reading of the gospel, by meditation on it, by its exhortations, threats, and promises, and also by the use of the sacraments.

Consider your state. You are a pardoned sinner, not under the law but under grace, freely, fully saved from the guilt of all your sins. There is none to condemn, God having justified you. He sees you in His Son, washed you in His blood, clothed you in His righteousness, and He embraces Him and you, the head and the members, with the same affection. - *William Romaine*

I rejoice in the hope of that glory to be revealed, for it is no uncertain glory that we look for. Our hope is not hung upon such an untwisted thread as, "I imagine so," or "It is likely," but the cable, the strong tow of our fastened anchor, is the oath and promise of Him who is eternal verity. Our salvation is fastened with God's own hand, and with Christ's own strength, to the strong stake of God's unchangeable nature.
- *Samuel Rutherford*

Faith is our seal; assurance of faith is God's seal. - *Christopher Nesse*

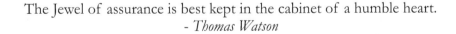

Assurance is a fruit that grows out of the root of faith; the fruits in Winter appear not upon the tree. Because I see not a flourishing top, shall I deny the existence and sappiness of the root? Mary, when she wept at Christ's feet, had no assurance of His love, yet Christ sends her away with the encomium of her faith, acted before the comfort dropped from His lips. - *Stephen Charnock*

The Jewel of assurance is best kept in the cabinet of a humble heart.
- *Thomas Watson*

DAY 6

ASSURANCE OF SALVATION
BY JOHN NEWTON

JESUS CHRIST THE LORD is a complete all-sufficient Savior. His invitation to the weary and heavy-laden is general, without exception, condition, or limitation. He has said, him who comes unto me, I will never cast out. God not only permits but commands us to believe in the Son of his love. The apostle affirms that He is able to save to the uttermost, all who come unto God by Him. When Moses raised the brazen serpent in the wilderness, the direction to the wounded Israelites was very short and simple: it was only, "*Look, and live!*" Thus the gospel addresses the sinner, "*Only believe, and you shall be saved.*"

Why then does not every sinner who is awakened to a sense of his guilt, danger, and helplessness, and whose desires are drawn towards the Savior, believe with full confidence, even upon his first application for mercy? Is not the remedy fully adequate to the malady? Is not the blood of Jesus able to cleanse from all sin? Is not the Word of the God of truth worthy of entire credit? Yet with such a Savior exhibited before the eyes of his mind, and with such promises sounding in his ears: he continues to hesitate and fluctuate between hope and fear. Could he rely as firmly on the Word of God, as he can on the word of a man, whom, he thinks, means what he says, and is able to make good his promises: he would immediately be filled with joy and peace in believing. But experience and observation may convince us, that, however rational and easy this assurance may seem in theory, it is ordinarily unattainable in practice: without passing through a train of previous exercises and conflicts.

It is true, young converts are often favored with comfortable impressions, which lead them to hope that their doubts and difficulties are already ended when perhaps they are but just entering upon their warfare.

They are brought, as it were, into a new world; a strong and lively sense of divine things engrosses their attention; the world and its fascinations sink into nothing in their esteem; the evil propensities which discourage them are overpowered for a season, and they hope they are quite subdued, and will trouble them no more. Their love, gratitude, praise, and admiration, are in vigorous exercise. An aged, experienced Christian may recollect, with a pleasing regret, many sweet sensations of this kind, in the early stages of his profession, which he cannot recall. But he now knows that the strong confidence he felt in these golden hours was not the assurance of faith. It was temporary and transient; it was founded upon what we call a good frame. Though his comforts were strong, his faith was weak; for, when the good frame subsided, his fears returned, his hope declined, and he was at his wits' end. Then, perhaps, he wondered at his own presumption, for daring to hope that such a creature as himself could have any right to the privileges of a believer. And if, in the warmth of his heart, he had spoken to others of what God had done for his soul, he afterwards charged himself with being a hypocrite, and a false witness both to God and man. Thus, when the Israelites saw the Egyptians, (who had pursued and terrified them,) cast up dead upon the shore of the Red Sea, they praised the Lord, and believed. They were little aware of the wilderness they had to pass through, and the trials they were to meet with before they could enter the promised land! But strong faith, and the effect of it, an abiding persuasion of our acceptance in the Beloved, and of our final perseverance in grace, are not necessarily connected with sensible comfort.

A strong faith can trust God in the dark, and say with Job, "Though he slays me, yet will I trust in him."

Yet it is not to be maintained without a diligent use of the instituted means of grace, and a conscientious attention to the precepts of the gospel. For mere notions of truth, destitute of power, will not keep the heart in peace. But this power depends upon the influence of the Holy Spirit; and if he is grieved by the willful commission of sin, or the willful neglect of the precepts. He hides his face, suspends his influence, and then confidence must proportionable decline, until he is pleased to return and revive it.

There are likewise bodily disorders, which, by depressing the physical spirits, darken and discolor the medium of our perceptions. If the enemy is permitted to take advantage of these seasons, he can pour in a flood of temptations, sufficient to fill the most assured believer with terror and dismay. But, ordinarily, those who endeavor to walk closely and conscientiously with God, attain, in due time, an assurance of hope to the end, which is not easily nor often shaken, though it is not absolutely perfect, nor can be, while so much sin and imperfection remain in us. If it be inquired WHY we cannot attain to this state of composure at first, since the object of faith and the promises of God are always the same? Several reasons may be assigned:

UNBELIEF is the primary cause of all our inquietude, from the moment that our hearts are drawn to seek salvation by Jesus. This inability to take God at his Word, should not be merely lamented as an infirmity but watched, and prayed, and fought against as a great sin. A great sin indeed it is; the very root of our apostasy, from which every other sin proceeds. Unbelief often deceives us under the guise of humility, as though it would be presumption, in such sinners as we are, to believe the declarations of the God of truth. Many serious people, who are burdened with a sense of other sins, leave this radical evil, unbelief, out of their list of sin. They rather indulge it, and think they ought not to believe, until they can find a warrant from marks and evidences within themselves.

But this is an affront to the wisdom and goodness of God, who points out to us the Son of His love as our wisdom, righteousness, sanctification, and redemption, without any regard to what we have been, or to what we are, excepting that broken and contrite spirit: which only Himself can create in us. And this broken spirit, though unbelief perverts it to our discouragement, is the very temper in which the Lord delights, and a surer evidence of true grace, than those which we are apt to contrive for ourselves. It is written, He who believes not the record which God has given of His Son, makes Him a liar. Why do we not startle with horror at the workings of unbelief, as we should do at a suggestion to commit murder, or the grossest outward enormity?

Again, our **NATURAL PRIDE** is a great hindrance to true faith. If we acknowledge ourselves to be sinners, and are sensible of our need of mercy, we are not easily brought to see that we are so totally depraved, so exceedingly vile, so utterly destitute of all good, as the Word of God describes us to be. A secret dependence upon our prayers, tears, resolutions, repentance and endeavors, prevents us from looking solely and simply to the Savior, so as to ground our whole hope for acceptance upon his obedience unto death, and his whole mediation.

A true believer will doubtless repent and pray, and forsake his former evil ways, but he is not accepted upon the account of what he does or feels but because Jesus lived and died, and rose and reigns on the behalf of sinners, and because he is enabled by grace to trust in him for salvation. Further, pride leads us into that spirit of vain reasoning, which is contrary to the simplicity of living by faith. Until this is renounced, until we become in some measure like little children, and receive the doctrines of Scripture implicitly, because they are from God, requiring no further proof of any point than a Thus says the Lord, we cannot be established in our hope.

Naaman was very desirous to be healed of his leprosy; but, if the Lord had not mercifully overruled his prejudices, he would have returned a leper just as he came. Before he went to Elisha, he had considered in his own mind, how the prophet ought to treat him; and not having the immediate attention paid to him that he expected, he was upon the point of going away; for his reason told him, that, if washing could affect his cure, the waters of Syria were as good as those of Jordan. "It seems," to use the words of a late ingenious writer, "that the gospel is too good to be believed, and too plain to be understood, until our pride is abased."

It is difficult to determine, by the eye, the precise moment of day-break, but the light advances from early dawn, and the sun arises at the appointed hour. Such is the progress of divine light in the mind, the first streaks of the dawn are seldom perceived; but, by degrees, objects, until then unthought of, are revealed. The evil of sin, the danger of the soul, the reality and importance of eternal things are apprehended, and a hope of mercy through a Savior is discovered, which prevents the sinner from sinking into absolute despair. But for a time, all is indistinct and confused.

In this state of mind, many things are anxiously sought for as prerequisites to believing, but they are sought in vain, for it is only by believing that they can be obtained. But the light increases, the sun arises, the glory of God in the person of Jesus Christ shines in upon the soul. As the sun can only be seen by its own light, and diffuses that light by which other objects are clearly perceived; so Christ crucified is the sun in the system of revealed truth; and the right knowledge of the doctrine of his cross satisfies the inquiring mind, proves itself to be the one thing needful, and the only thing necessary to silence the objections of unbelief and pride, and to afford a sure ground for solid and abiding hope.

Once more, we cannot be safely trusted with assurance until we have that knowledge of the evil and deceitfulness of our hearts, which can be acquired only by painful, repeated experience. The young convert, in his brighter hours, when his heart is full of joys, and he thinks his mountain stands too strong to be removed, may be compared to a ship with much sail spread, and but little ballast. She goes on well while the weather is fair but is not prepared for a storm. When Peter said, "You have the words of eternal life, we believe and are sure that you are the Christ," and when he protested, "Though all men should forsake you, yet will not I," he undoubtedly spoke honestly; but the event showed that he did not know himself! His resolution was soon and sorely shaken in the hall of the high-priest, so that he denied his Lord with oaths and imprecations. He was left to fall that he might learn he did not stand by his own strength.

The parable of the prodigal may be accommodated for an illustration of this point. The Scripture says, "Then shall you know if you follow on to know the Lord." But we often want to know at first, and at once; and suppose if I was but sure that I am right, and accepted in the Beloved, I could go on with more spirit and success. Many rejoice greatly when they seem to obtain this desire but their joy is short-lived. They soon resemble the prodigal; they become vain, rash, and careless; they forsake their Father's house; their attention to the means of grace is slackened; they venture upon smaller deviations from the prescribed rule, which, in time, lead them to greater.

Thus their stock of grace and comfort is quickly exhausted. They begin to be in need; and, after having been feasted with the bread of life, are reduced to feed upon such husks as the world can afford them. Happy, if at length they are brought to their right minds!

But, oh, with what pungent shame and humiliation do they come back to their Father! He, indeed, is always ready to receive and forgive backsliders; but surely they cannot easily forgive themselves for their ingratitude and folly! When he has healed their broken bones, and restored peace to their souls, it may be expected that they will walk softly and humbly to the end of their days, and not open their mouths any more, either to boast, or to censure, or to complain!

For, a man who possesses a Scriptural and well-grounded assurance in himself will evidence it to others by suitable fruits. He will be meek, sincere and gentle in his conduct before men because he is humbled and abased before God. Because he lives upon much God's forgiveness to himself, he will be ready to forgive others. The prospect of that blessed hope assuredly laid up for him in heaven will make him patient under all his appointed trials in the present life, wean him from an attachment to the world, and preserve him from being much affected either by the smiles or the frowns of mortals. To hear people talk much of their "assurance," and that they are freed from all doubts and fears while they habitually indulge proud, angry, resentful, discontented tempers, or while they are eagerly grasping after the world, like those who seek their whole portion in it, is painful and disgusting to a serious Christian! Let us pity them, and pray for them; for we have great reason to fear that they do not understand what they say, nor what they affirm!

He that believeth on Jesus shall never be confounded. Never was any; neither shall you, if you believe. It was a great word of faith spoken by a dying man, who had been converted in a singular way, betwixt his condemnation and execution: his last words were these, spoken with a mighty shout, "never man perished with his face towards Jesus Christ."
- Robert Traill

We count it no presumption to say that we are saved, for the Word of God has told us so in those places where salvation is promised to faith in Christ. The presumption would lie in doubting the Word of God.
- C.H. Spurgeon

Assurance is, as it were, the cream of faith. - *William Gurnall*

Full assurance that Christ hath delivered Paul from condemnation, yea, so full and real as produceth thanksgiving and triumphing in Christ, may and doth consist with complaints and out-cries of a wretched condition for the indwelling of the body of sin. - *Samuel Rutherford*

Assurance is our reaction to the gift of salvation and our reflection on our trust in Christ. - *Sinclair Ferguson*

DAY 7

CHRISTIAN HOPE
BY JOHN ANGELL JAMES

WHY IS IT, that so few professors of true religion, and even true Christians, enjoy and exhibit so little of that joy and peace in believing, which the New Testament declares to be their privilege, and which, it might be supposed, their state and condition warrant and demand? That the great mass of professors do appear destitute of this spiritual delight is too notorious to be denied. In affliction are they not as disconsolate as other men? Do not their troubles put out the lights of their comfort, and cause them to walk in darkness? In prosperity, how little of their happiness is derived from spiritual sources. The springs of their felicity lie in earthly, rather than in heavenly things. How rare is the case of one whose countenance is generally illuminated with a smile, and that smile the reflection of the beams of the Sun of Righteousness. How is this? Why is it that we do not let the light of our joy, as well as of our holiness, shine before men, and thus let our personal history stand as the index that points to the fountain of bliss? Why?

Because so many professing Christians, to allude to Bunyan's immortal allegory, are imprisoned in "Doubting Castle." How few are there who, if the question were proposed to them, "Are you assured you are a child of God?" would answer even in this modest language, "I believe I am, and am happy in this delightful persuasion." The greater number would hesitate, and tell you plainly and at once, that they have their doubts and fears about this matter, and cannot really persuade themselves that this is their state. Ought this to be so? Ought a real Christian to be in constant, serious doubt whether he is a Christian? The change produced by the converting grace of God might be supposed, from its nature and greatness, to be its own evidence. It is a change in a man's whole moral nature, if indeed, it really exists. It is a change so accurately described in the Word of God, that anyone who will deal honestly with himself, look into his own heart, consult his own consciousness, and compare himself with the Word of God, might know his state. The features of a child of God and of a child of the devil, are not so like each other as to be hardly distinguished.

And as reason would lead us to conclude, the state of grace may be distinguished from a state of nature; the Scriptures everywhere assert that it may be, and suppose that it is. "We know that we have passed from death unto life," says the apostle, "because we love the brethren," 1 John 3:14. And in a subsequent passage of the same epistle, the apostle says, "These things have I written unto you who believe on the name of the Son of God, that you may know that you have eternal life," chap. 5:13.

Would it not appear strange if there were really no means of knowing that we had really become Christians?

How could it be said God was "more abundantly willing that we should have strong consolation," if we could have no knowledge he had forgiven our sins and received us to favor, until we reached the heavenly country? It is not only represented as possible that we may obtain this blessed knowledge now but it is actually made a duty to seek it. "And we desire," says the apostle, "that every one of you show the same diligence to the full assurance of hope unto the end," Heb. 6:11.

The state of mind here enjoined is not only hope, but the assurance of hope; not, only the assurance, but the full assurance. This, observe, is not merely held out as a privilege, but enjoined as a duty; and not only a duty for some, but for everyone; and a state not occasional, but habitual, not for a time, but "unto the end." This is in accordance with what another apostle enjoins "therefore brethren, give diligence to make your calling and election sure," 2 Peter 1:10. That is, sure to ourselves. Let it then be distinctly understood that assurance is not only the privilege of a few but the duty of all. And yet how few enjoy it. Why?

Ignorance of its nature keeps many from it. Hence the necessity of explanation. There are three kinds of assurance spoken of in the New Testament;

1. "The full assurance of **understanding**," Col. 2:2. This means a clear, comprehensive, and soul-establishing acquaintance with divine truth.

2. "The full assurance of **faith**," Heb. 10:22. By this we are to understand a strong, settled, unwavering conviction of the truth of the gospel.

3. "The full assurance of **hope**." These three are intimately connected with each other, and one rises out of the other.

Here is first a clear understanding of the gospel, then a firm belief of what is so understood, and then the hope of what is believed; a personal *knowledge*, a personal *belief*, a personal *hope*. And the reason why many do not possess the last, is that they do not clearly see, and constantly remember, that it can be obtained only by the two preceding ones.

But what is the true nature of this assurance of hope? It must be distinctly borne in mind, that it is only the assurance of hope, not of possession. Let hope be as confident as it may, it is still but hope, and cannot have all the undoubting and absolute certainty of possession. The latter leaves no room for doubt or fear. The former may. By the state of mind therefore indicated by the phrase I am now considering, it is not meant that it consists in the Christian's being able to feel and to say he is as certain of getting to heaven as if he were already there. It is not meant that he possesses such an absolute and undoubting certainty as admits of no degrees; much less a kind of boastful, ostentatious, and vainglorious confidence of safety.

It may be expressed thus: "The Word of God tells me that he who believes in Christ shall be saved; I am conscious that I have believed in Christ and have thus committed my soul to him; therefore I believe my sins are forgiven, and I hope for eternal salvation. I have such a persuasion of the reality of my faith, therefore of the pardon of my sins, and reconciliation to God, that I have no serious doubt of my being a child of God and an heir of glory." This I call assurance; such a persuasion of our having received the grace of God in our hearts, as excludes distressing doubts and fears.

Still, it is such a persuasion of our being true believers, as admits of degrees, for we find it so stated in the different passages which refer to it; we have "assurance," "full assurance," and "much full assurance," clearly proving, I repeat, that the word imports a state of mind which admits of various degrees of certainty. Of the very people who are represented as having "much full assurance," the apostle says that their "faith grew exceedingly," 1 Thess. 1:5. But if assurance meant a state of mind that entirely and forever excluded all doubt, how could it grow beyond full assurance?

I therefore again say that the Scripture does not warrant us to describe it as going beyond a pleasing and satisfactory conclusion that we have passed from death unto life; which, after all, is very different from that certainty which accompanies possession. How else can we harmonize it with the exhortation to "work out our salvation with fear and trembling," or with the other admonition to "fear, lest a promise being left us of entering into his rest, any of us should seem to come short of it." There is a wide difference between possessing a calm and comfortable enjoyment of this persuasion of true faith and being forward to affirm it, and to glory in it before others. A believer may be in the full possession of an inward, tranquil, and even joyful persuasion of his state before God, and of his safety for eternity; and yet not stand ready when the question, "are you sure you are a child of God?" is put to him by a fellow creature, to reply with an unhesitating boldness, "I am as sure of it as if I heard a voice from heaven declare it." The right answer to such a question is the following, "I am a poor, sinful, guilty, lost creature - worthless, helpless, hopeless. But I believe the record God has given of his Son. On him, as the true and only foundation, I place all my hopes of eternal life, and I have therefore joy and peace in believing. Christ is my all. His finished work is the sole ground of my confidence. I think I am accepted by God. I know whom I have believed, and am persuaded he is able to keep that which I have committed to him against that day. O, to grace how great a debtor I am."

This I consider the scriptural assurance. It may fall short of the boast of some but it accords best with the Word of God, and with the experience of God's saints in general. It is a knowledge that we have passed from death to life though it is a knowledge which is less than that of the absolute and undoubting certainty which some contend for.

This is a blessed state of mind, and much to be desired. How blessed to have the great question thus satisfactorily settled, and to be relieved from painful solicitude and distressing fear about our safety for eternity. What, compared with this, is it to have fears about our health, or property, or liberty, or even life, removed? How great, how pure the joy afforded by such a persuasion as this, "Yes, I think I am a believer in Christ, a converted man, a child of God, an heir of glory, a traveler to heaven. I can say, with unfaltering tongue, O God, you are my God. Blessed Jesus, you know all things, you know that I love you."

O, what sunshine does such a persuasion throw over the landscape of life, illumining its barren wastes, and bringing out all the beauty, and verdure, and bloom of its Paradisaic spots. What privations may we not endure, what afflictions may we not bear, when we can say, "God is my Father, Christ my Savior, salvation my portion, and heaven my home!" This has carried consolation into the darkest recesses of human woe, the lowest depths of poverty and need. With this, confessors have made the walls of their prison echo with their songs, and martyrs have been happy on the scaffold and at the stake. With this, we may live in happiness and die in peace. It is a jewel worth infinitely more than all the gems which have ever blazed on beauty or royalty.

The man who can rejoice in saying he is a Christian in reality, need not sigh over anything else that he is not.

We shall never have it, if we do not desire it. Surely if anything be desirable, it must be, or ought to be, this. The absence of all solicitude about such a matter indicates either the total lack, or the great weakness, of personal, vital religion. That they who are altogether careless about true religion should never trouble themselves about the matter, is natural enough but that professors of religion should be indifferent to it, is indeed for a marvel. And yet, I fear it is a subject about which the great bulk of them give themselves no concern. Ask them if they have any good ground to conclude they are the children of God, and are living in the happy persuasion they are safe for eternity, and in multitudes of instances, they will tell you they really do not know, and tell it almost with such an air of levity, as too plainly shows how little interest they take in true religion altogether. Such people may well doubt of their state; they have good reason to doubt. Indifference to the question, "Am I indeed a child of God?" is a sad and sure indication of an unchanged heart. But even pious people are not so earnest about this matter as they ought to be. With them it is too generally left undecided, and in many cases because undesired.

Is it not to be coveted that we should go on our way rejoicing to everlasting glory? Is it not desirable that, like Bunyan's Pilgrim, we should get out of Doubting Castle and repose amid the beauties of the Delectable Mountains of assurance?

Assurance does not lie in what we are, be we great or small. It lies in what God has done in his plan of salvation to secure us to himself.
- *Sinclair Ferguson*

There is no better assurance of salvation to he found anywhere than can he gained from the decree of God. - *John Calvin*

Assurance makes heavy afflictions light, long afflictions short, bitter afflictions sweet. - *Thomas Brooks*

When we speak of the grounds of assurance, we are thinking of the ways in which a believer comes to entertain this assurance, not of the grounds on which his salvation rests. The grounds of salvation are as secure for the person who does not have full assurance as for the person who has.
- *John Murray*

It is not faith that saves, but faith in Jesus Christ... It is not, strictly speaking, even faith in Christ that saves, but Christ that saves through faith. The saving power resides exclusively, not in the act of faith or the attitude of faith or the nature of faith, but in the object of faith... Christ Himself. - *B.B. Warfield*

DAY 8

THOUGHTS ON THE ASSURANCE OF FAITH
BY AUGUSTUS TOPLADY

IT HAS LONG BEEN a settled point with me, that the Scriptures make a wide distinction between faith, the assurance of faith, and the full assurance of faith.

ONE: Faith is the hand by which we embrace or touch, or reach toward, the garment of Christ's righteousness, for our own justification. Such a soul is undoubtedly safe.

TWO: Assurance I consider as the ring which God puts, upon faith's finger. Such a soul is not only safe, but also comfortable and happy. Assurance after it has been vouchsafed to the soul may be lost. Peter no doubt lost his assurance, and sinned it away, when he denied Christ. He did not, however, lose the principle of faith; for Christ had before-hand prayed, concerning him, that his faith itself might not fail: and Christ could not possibly pray in vain. A wife may lose her wedding-ring. But that does not dissolve her marriage relation. She continues a lawful wife still. And yet she is not easy until she find her ring again.

THREE: Full assurance I consider as the brilliant, or cluster of brilliants, which adorns the ring, and renders it incomparably more beautiful and valuable. Where the diamond of full assurance is thus set in the gold of faith, it diffuses its rays of love, joy, peace, and holiness, with a lustre which leaves no room for doubt or darkness. While these high and unclouded consolations remain, the believer's felicity is only inferior to that of angels, or of saints made perfect above.

FOUR: After all, I apprehend that the very essence of assurance lies in communion with God. While we feel the sweetness of his inward presence, we cannot doubt of our interest in his tender mercies. So long as the Lord speaks comfortably to our hearts, our affections are on fire, our views are clear, and our faces shine. It is when we come down from the mount, and when we mix with the world again, that we are in danger of losing that precious sense of his love, which is the strength of saint's militant, and the joy of souls triumphant.

But let not trembling believers forget that faith, strictly so called, is neither more nor less than a receiving of Christ, for ourselves in particular, as our only possible propitiation, righteousness, and Saviour: John i. 12. - Hast thou so received Christ? Thou art a believer, to all the purposes of safety. And it deserves special notice that our Lord calls the centurion's faith "great faith;" though it rose no higher than to make him say "Speak the word only, and my servant shall be healed." Matt. viii. 8-10.

The case likewise of the Canaanitish woman is full to the present point. Her cry was, "Have mercy on me, O Lord, thou Son of David!" And, a little after, "Lord, help me!" Jesus at first gave her a seeming repulse: but her importunity continued, and she requested only the privilege of a dog, viz., to eat of the crumbs which fell from the master's table. What were our Saviour's answer and our Saviour's remark? An answer and a remark which ought to make every broken sinner take down his harp from the willows: "O woman, great is thy faith." Matt. x. 22-28.

FIVE: The graces which the blessed Spirit implants in our hearts (and the grace of faith among the rest) resemble a sun-dial; which is of little service except when the sun shines upon it. The Holy Ghost must shine upon the graces he has given, or they will leave us at a loss (in point of spiritual comfort), and be unable to tell us where-abouts we are. May he, day by day, rise upon our souls with healing in his beams! Then shall we be filled with all joy and peace in believing, and abound in hope, through the power of the Holy Ghost. Rom. xv. 13.

SIX: Are there any weak in faith who come under the denomination of bruised reeds and smoking flax? Let them know that God will take care of them. The former will not be broken: the latter shall not be quenched. Bless God for any degree of faith; even though it be as the smallest of all seeds, sooner or later it will surely expand into a large and fruitful tree. However, stop not here; but, as the apostle advises, covet earnestly the best gifts: and the gift of assurance, yea, of fullest assurance among the rest. The stronger you are in faith, the more glory you will give to God, both in lip and life. Lord, increase our faith! Amen.

We should all be concerned about our assurance of salvation, because if we lack assurance we lack joy, and if we lack joy our life is of probably poor quality. - *D.M. Lloyd-Jones*

Let thy eye and heart, first, most, and last, be fixed upon Christ, then will assurance bed and board with thee. - *Thomas Brooks*

There is no reason why weak believers should conclude against themselves. Weak faith unites as really with Christ as strong faith - as the least bud in the vine is drawing sap and life from the root, no less than the strongest branch. Weak believers therefore, have abundant cause to be thankful; and while they reach after growth in grace, ought not to overlook what they have already received. - *Henry Venn*

I was diverted from Christ for several years, to search only into the signs of grace in me. It was almost seven years ere I was taken off to live by faith on Christ, and God's free love, which are alike the object of faith. - *Thomas Goodwin*

A promise once given unto a soul, shall never be reversed or repealed and have ye not the whole gospel before you [as] a bag of golden promises? - *William Bridge*

DAY 9

KEPT BY THE POWER OF GOD
BY WILLIAM ROMAINE

*The believer, kept by the Power of God, perseveres in his holy walk
and victorious warfare.*

EVEN AFTER THE BELIEVER has made a great progress in his walk,
and has been very successful in his warfare, yet he is not out of the reach
of any temptation. He is still liable to be stopped in the way of his duty.
His enemies may cheat him by some stratagem, or gain some advantage
over him by open force. While he is attending to these things, as they
come before him in his daily experience, a thought will often arise...

> *I am afraid my profession will at last come to nothing, and I shall be cast
> away. I feel so much corruption working in my duties, and my heart is so
> ready to revolt and to turn from the Lord in every battle, that I cannot help
> being uneasy about my final state. How can I? It is not in me to hold out
> and persevere against so much opposition from within and without. What
> signifies my resolution to walk forward, or to fight for an uncertain crown? I
> think I gain no ground. My own carnal will plagues me, and I love ease and
> quiet as much as ever. My corruptions seem as many, and mine enemies as
> strong, as they were. One day, I fear, I shall perish by their hands. My heart
> faints at the thought. My courage fails me. O wretched man that I am!
> where, to whom shall I look for strength to enable me to hold out unto the
> end?*

No believer is absolutely free from such an attack; and there are seasons
very favourable to it. If his mind be in heaviness through manifold
temptations, and by reasoning legally upon them: if he be under the
hidings of the Lord's countenance, or in a time of desertion; if he be
fallen into any great sin, perhaps his old besetting sin; if the guilt of it be
upon his conscience, and the indignation of God be heavy upon him;
then such thoughts find easy admittance; and if they be indulged, they
greatly distress the believer; for they directly assault his faith, and strike at
the very being of his hope. As these graces are weakened, he moves
slowly; and if unbelief prevail, there is a stop put to his progress in the
heavenly road.

Blessed be the Lord God of Israel, who has made ample provision for
victory over this temptation. The principles before insisted on are now to
be brought into practice. Here is a fresh occasion to try their power and
influence, and to make it appear that in these distressing circumstances
the Father has given His children good ground to rely upon His
unchangeable love. He has revealed to them the immutability of His
counsel and of His oath, that when they have fled to Jesus for refuge,

they may comfort their hearts and say; I have been afraid of falling away, but it is without reason; for I have still immutable things to trust in although to my sense and feeling everything seems to make against me, yet God has promised not to leave me nor forsake me. O that I may honour His promise, and without doubting rely upon His faithful arm to make it good!

Consider then, O my soul, the principles of the doctrine of Christ. Review them carefully. Thou seest what influence they have upon every step of thy walk, and how mighty they are, through God, to carry thee through all thy difficulties. O study then the perfect freeness and the absolute sufficiency of the salvation of Jesus. Read and mark the bonds and securities which a faithful God has given thee to trust in, and not to be afraid. The time to honour them most is to believe them when thou hast the least sensible evidence, for that is the strongest faith. If thou canst believe upon His bare word, and it is a very good warrant, thy feet shall stand firm upon the rock, and thy goings shall be well ordered: and that thou mayest believe this in the hardest trials, God informs thee that thy continuance in grace does not depend on thyself.

"Thou standest by faith" and faith should direct thee to what God has undertaken and has promised to do for thee.

He would have thee to place the confidence of thy heart upon His tried word, which is a never-failing foundation, and if thou wast to build all thy hopes of persevering upon it, it would quiet thy fears and comfort thy heart. Thou wouldst then see that God has not left thee to thyself to stand or fall, but has engaged never to leave thee nor forsake thee. He has declared He will not turn away from thee to do thee good, and He will put His fear into thy heart, and thou shalt not turn away from Him. View thy case in this comfortable light, and while thou art considering the safety of thy persevering, as revealed in Scripture for the ground of thy faith, may every promise lead thee to trust more in God, and to trust less to thyself, and then the snare which was laid for thee will be broken, and thou wilt be delivered.

But take heed of carrying thine opinions to Scripture, and of forcing it to speak for them. Beware of that common mistake, and beware of human systems. Pay no regard to men or names. Simply attend to the promises of God concerning thy persevering. Thy present trial has convinced thee that thou canst not depend on thy own faithfulness; this therefore is the time to learn practically the faithfulness of God, and to improve thy faith in it from such Scripture arguments as these:

FIRST: The nature of the divine covenant, which is not only the unchangeable will of the eternal three, but is also their agreement, confirmed by oath, concerning the heirs of promise.

- ◆ **The Father** loved them as His children, freely, with an everlasting love. He chose them, and gave them to His Son. He engaged to keep them by His power, through faith unto salvation.

- ◆ **The Son** accepted them, and wrote all their names in His book (not one of them therefore can be lost); He undertook to be made man, and to live and die for them; to rise from the dead, to ascend, and to intercede for them; and He sitteth as King-Mediator upon the throne, till every one of them be brought to glory.

- ◆ **The Holy Spirit** covenanted to carry into execution the purposes of the Father's love, and to apply the blessings of the Son's salvation. He undertook to quicken the heirs of promise, to call them effectually, to guide, to strengthen, to sanctify, and to comfort them; yea, He is not to leave them, till the number of the elect be perfected. Therefore, He abides with them forever.

In this covenant the eternal Three have undertaken for every heir of promise to do all for him, and all in him, for the means and for the end, so that not one of them can perish; for faithfulness to the covenant is one of the highest honours of the Godhead: "I am Jehovah, which keepeth covenant; I will ever be mindful of My covenant. My covenant will I not break, nor alter the thing that has gone out of My mouth." What strong consolation is there in these words! Study them, O my soul, that by them thy faith may be established, and they may do thee good, like a medicine.

Thou art afraid of falling away; but the blessed Trinity have undertaken to hold thee up, and Their covenant engagements are to be the ground of thy believing that They will fulfil what They have promised. Observe and adore the goodness of God. See how He meets thy doubts and answers thy objections: "An oath for confirmation is to them an end of all strife: wherein God, willing more abundantly to show to the heirs of promise the immutability of His counsel, confirmed it by an oath that by two immutable things, in which it was impossible for God to lie, we might have a strong consolation, who have fled for refuge" to Jesus. Thy faith should run parallel with this promise, and should safely trust as far as it warrants thee; now it gives thee sufficient reason to conclude that thy state before God is immutable, and that He has determined thou shalt not fall away and perish. For observe,

SECONDLY: His design in the covenant.

He knew thy frame, thy infirmities, and thy temptation, and therefore He provided the covenant, and promised the blessings of it upon oath for thy sake, to end all strife in thy conscience, and to give thee strong consolation. This was His mind and will. He revealed it for thee, to settle thy heart in believing, and to administer to thee great comfort. Weigh attentively each of these particulars, and then say what more could have been done to satisfy thee of thine immutable persevering.

But thou thinkest such trials as thine are uncommon, and perhaps not provided for in the covenant, and therefore it can be no disparagement to the divine faithfulness if thou shouldst fall away. How can this be, since the everlasting covenant is ordered in all things, and on the part of God is absolutely sure? Nothing that concerns thee is left out of it, not a single hair of thy head; thy trials are all appointed and ordered, and the end also which they are to answer.

Perhaps, from the clear evidence of the divine Record, thou art convinced of the covenant of God to save the heir of promise, and of His engaging to keep them that they shall never perish; but thou art afraid thou art not in the covenant, nor an heir of promise. From whence arise thy fears? From Scripture? No! All Scripture is on thy side. Hast thou not fled as a poor sinner to Jesus for refuge? Hast thou not acknowledged His divine nature, and His all-sufficient work? And though thou art now tempted to doubt, yet some faith is still fighting against unbelief. These are covenant blessings. O look up, then, to Jesus; why not thy Jesus? But, however, look to Him, keep looking on and He will give thee reason to be ashamed of thy doubts and fears.

"But the Lord hides Himself from me, and therefore I fear I am not in His favour." This objection is answered in the charter of grace: "I will not turn away from doing thee good." He has hidden His face, and thou art troubled; this trouble is for good. It should put thee upon inquiring into the reason for God's hiding Himself. It should humble thee, and should exercise thy faith upon such a scripture as this: "For the iniquity of his covetousness was I wroth; and smote him; I hid Me, and was wroth, and he went on frowardly in the way of his heart. I have seen his ways and will heal him; I will lead him also, and will restore comforts to him and to his mourners." Although He hid Himself, yet He had love to His people; although He smote them, yet it was with a Fatherly correction.

But, thou fearest God not only hides His face, but has also quite forsaken thee. He may, as to thy sense and feeling, but not as to His own purpose, which changeth not. Hear how He speaks to thee, and silences thy doubts: "For a small moment have I forsaken thee, but with great mercies will I gather thee: in a little wrath I hid My face from thee for a moment, but with everlasting kindness will I have mercy on thee, saith the Lord Thy Redeemer." How gracious is thy God! What infinite mercy is it, that He should give thee such promises, so suited to the trials of thy faith, to preserve thee under them, and to bring thee out of them!

Read carefully over and over again these promises, and may every reading of them disperse the cloud of unbelief, until thy soul be enlivened with the light of the Lord's loving countenance.

But perhaps thou art in a worse case as to thine own apprehension. Thou thinkest: "God is incensed against me, and justly; He has cast me off, and I can expect no more favour at His hand. Once, indeed, I thought He loved me, but I have fallen into a great sin, an old besetting sin; my conscience accuses me of committing it against light and conviction; it is a foul, black spot, such as is not to be found upon the children of God."

Thou art fallen, and wilt thou lie there, and not be raised up again? Thou art under guilt, and wilt thou nurse it, and add sin to sin? Aggravate the sinfulness of thy fall as much as thou wilt, yet thou canst not be truly humbled for it but by returning to God, and by trusting in the plenteous redemption that is in Christ Jesus. Then thy heart will be softened and melted into love, for grace will have its due honour, and thou wilt see what the Scripture says of thy case, in its divine truth and majesty. Thou wilt feel thyself exactly what the Word of God says of thee, a fallen sinful creature; in thee (that is, in thy flesh) dwelleth no good thing; so that there is not any sin but thou art capable of falling into it, through the strength of temptation. So long as thou art in the body, the flesh lusteth against the spirit, and the spirit against the flesh; in this conflict thou mayest fall, but the covenant secures thee from perishing.

Abraham, the father of the faithful, fell, the friend of God fell into the same sin again and again. Moses fell; so did David. Peter, forewarned, fell; so did all the apostles. Yet they were believers, and they recovered themselves out of the snare of the devil. For whatever sin thou art fallen into may be pardoned, as theirs was. "The blood of Jesus Christ cleanseth from all sin:" there is in it an infinite virtue to wash away every spot and stain; it is a public fountain; it stands open for daily use, that believers may wash and be clean; it is always, at every given moment, effectual; it cleanseth, in the present tense, now, today, while it is called today, for there is nothing new to be suffered on the part of Christ, in order to take away sin. He put it away by the sacrifice of Himself, the Father accepted it, and thus proclaims the free forgiveness of all the trespasses for which the atonement was made: "I will be merciful to their unrighteousness, and their sins and their iniquities will I remember no more." Why dost thou reject the comfort of this promise? It is suited to thy present distress, and is the remedy for it. Thou art fallen into unrighteousness; God says, I will be merciful to it. Thou art fallen into sins and iniquities; He says, I will remember them no more. Thou mayest remember thy fall, but let it be in order to rise from it by faith. It should teach thee thy need of the blood of the Lamb. It should bring thee to sprinkle it afresh upon thy conscience, and to live safe and happy under the protection of it. Thus apply it to thy fall, and thou wilt repent aright;

thou wilt be truly humbled and made more watchful. Thou wilt live more by faith in thy covenant God, wilt glorify more the infinitely perfect salvation of Jesus, and wilt be more dependent upon the grace and keeping of the eternal Spirit.

Consider then, O my soul, the rich, abounding, super-abounding grace of thy God, in making such a provision for raising thee up when fallen into sin. He intended the promises in the covenant should be the means of thy recovery, as they give thee good ground still to trust in a covenant God, and in His immutable counsel and oath. O lie not then in guilt, rest not in unbelief, give not place to the devil. The Lord has put words into thy mouth, may He help thee, in the faith of thy heart, to take them up and say, "Rejoice not against me, O mine enemy; when I fall, I shall arise; when I sit in darkness, the Lord shall be a light unto me. I will bear the indignation of the Lord, because I have sinned against Him, until He plead my cause, and execute judgment for me; He will bring me forth to the light, and I shall behold His righteousness." If the Lord open to thee the rich treasury of grace in this scripture, and enable thee to depend on the ample security here given for raising thee from thy fall, then consider, in the

THIRD PLACE: The express promises made in the covenant, that the believer shall not perish, but shall have everlasting life.

These promises are not conditional, made to the believer upon certain terms, as if upon doing his part God would do His also; for he does not stand by his own will, or strength, or faithfulness; he does not hold out to the end by his own diligence and watchfulness in means, or receive the crown of glory as the merited reward of any works of righteousness done by him; the promises are all of free grace, not dependent on man's will, but on God's; not yea and nay, but of absolutely certain fulfilment. They were all made in the covenant to Christ the Head, and are already made good to Christ, as the Head, for the use of His members. "For all the promises of God are in Him, yea, and in Him amen." He was given for the covenant of His people, and as such He undertook to do all their works for them and in them, and therefore all the promised blessings of the covenant are laid up in His fulness. "In Him they are yea" and laid up, as the head has the fulness of the senses for the use of its members, "in Him they are Amen." He communicates the promised blessings freely, not conditionally; by believing, and not for working. "Therefore," says the apostle, speaking of Christ's righteousness, "it is of faith, that it might be by grace, to the end the promise might be sure to all the seed."

In this sovereign manner and style runs the covenant, and every promise in it: I will be their God, of Mine own mere motion and grace, and according to the good pleasure of Mine own will, and they shall be My people. My will shall make them willing in the day of My power: for I will work in them both to will and to do; yea, I will be a Father unto them, and they shall be My sons and daughters, saith the Lord Almighty. The word Father relates to His children, and expresses the unchangeable love of His heart towards them; it is a dear covenant name, and denotes the inseparable connection between Him and His children; whenever they hear it, it should always excite in them an idea of His everlasting affection. He loves His family as a Father, and loves every one of them with the same almighty love. He cannot change. He cannot cease to be a Father, and they cannot cease to be His children. His name is a security to them, that they cannot perish, for if one of them could, they all might. And then His covenant purpose to bring many sons unto glory would be defeated, His relation to them as a Father would be broken, He would be a Father without children, He would deny them the promised blessings, He would forget to be gracious to them, His will concerning them would change, or would be overruled by some opposite will, and His great plan in the covenant would come to nothing.

But these things cannot possibly be. He is the Father of His children, and He has engaged, by promise and oath, to love, to bless, and to keep them forever. Out of perfect love He gave them to His Son, who undertook to be their Saviour; He came and was made man, Jehovah incarnate, to live and die for them. He was so delighted with them (for He has all their names written in His book), and with the work, that He was straitened till it was accomplished. Blessings on Him forever! It is finished. The royal Saviour is upon the throne, almighty to save His dear redeemed.

He would lose His name, which is above every name, the honours of His salvation would fade away upon His head, and the glories of His offices would come to nothing, if one, whom Jesus lived and died to save, should perish. But it is not possible. Whom He loves, He loves unto the end.

"I give unto them," says He, "eternal life; and they shall never perish, neither shall any pluck them out of My hand." They are His seed, and it was covenanted that He should see His seed. They are the travail of His soul, and He shall see of the travail of His soul, and shall be satisfied. How can He be satisfied, if any one of them should be lost? He prayed, "Holy Father, keep through Thine own name those whom Thou hast given Me, that they may be one, as We are One." And the Father always heard Him. He prayed that they might be with Him where He is, to see His glory: and the Holy Spirit covenanted to bring them to it, He undertook, as His name, Spirit, imports, to breathe life into them, to call, to convert them, to keep them, and to give them everything needful for their spiritual life. How can they fail of coming to glory, being thus kept for it by the power of God? The Holy Spirit would lose His name, Spirit, or breath of life, and His office, which is to abide with, and to dwell forever in, the elect people of God, if any one of them should die from God, and perish. Thus there is full security given by the names and offices of the Trinity, that believers shall be kept from falling away.

- ♦ The **Father** cannot be without His children.

- ♦ The glory of **Jesus** would fade away if one of His redeemed was plucked out of His hand.

- ♦ The divine honours of the **Spirit** of life would be eclipsed if He was to forsake His charge, and suffer any of the redeemed to fall into hell.

But these things cannot be. The will of the Father, Son, and Spirit is the same concerning the salvation of the elect, which is as secure as covenant bonds and oaths can make it.

Art thou then, O my soul, established in this great truth? Dost thou yield to the power of the evidence which the blessed Trinity have vouchsafed to give thee? Meditate carefully upon it for the growth of thy faith. Search the Scriptures, and observe how clearly God declares His fixed purpose to keep His people, and to hold them up unto the end. The great preacher of the gospel in the Old Testament Church speaks thus of the unchangeable will of a covenant God: "The mountains shall depart, and the hills be removed, but My kindness shall not depart from thee, neither shall the covenant of My peace be removed, saith the Lord that hath mercy on thee."

A great preacher in the New Testament Church has confirmed the same precious truth. He is speaking of the golden chain of salvation, and showing how inseparable every link of it is, and in this prospect he triumphs: "Who shall lay anything to the charge of God's elect? It is God that justifieth, who is he that condemneth? It is Christ that died, yea, rather, that is risen again, who is even at the right hand of God, who also maketh intercession for us. Who shall separate us from the love of Christ? Shall tribulation, or distress, or persecution, or famine, or nakedness, or sword? Nay, in all these things we are more than conquerors through Him that loved us." By the mouth of these two infallible witnesses the truth is established. They depose that the covenant is immutable, and that nothing can separate believers from the love wherewith God loves them in His Son. O most comfortable doctrine! How encouraging is it in any undertaking to set about it with certain hope of success. How animating in our Christian walk, how reviving in the dark and difficult path of it, to have God's promise that He will keep us, and bring us to a happy end. How pleasing is it to go on by faith in our warfare, casting all our care upon Him who careth for us. How delightful is it to trust His promise, and daily to find it made good:

"Ye are kept by the power of God, through faith, unto eternal salvation." Here, O my soul, thou art to seek for strong consolation amidst the trials and difficulties of thy walk. Thou art afraid of falling, God has engaged to hold thee up. Thou hast been tempted to think thou shouldst fall quite away, and come to nothing; but God says, thou art preserved in Christ Jesus. His covenant and oath are made to confirm the faith of thy persevering. Thou standest by faith, and thy faith should lead thee to rest safely on what God says about thy standing; and for thy faith itself, its continuing, its increasing, thou hast His infallible faithfulness to depend upon.

Thou art weak, but He keeps thee by His power. Thine enemies are strong but none of them shall pluck thee out of His hand. Thou art willing to join them, and to depart from the living God, but He has promised to put His fear into thy heart, and thou shalt not depart from Him. He meets with thy doubts, and answers all thine objections in a word: "For He hath said, I will never leave thee, nor forsake thee."

Be of good courage, then, O my soul, and go forward, strong in the Lord, and in the power of His might, and He will bring thee safe to the end of thy journey.

He has promised it. Put thyself into His hands, and give Him the glory of keeping thee. He will hold up thy goings in His paths, that thy footsteps slip not. The Lord shall preserve thee from all evil. The Lord shall preserve thy going out and thy coming in, from this time forth, and even for evermore. How then canst thou miscarry, safe under His guidance and keeping? Commit thy ways unto the Lord. Do it simply. Look up by faith to His promise, and then lean on His arm. Thus going on thou mayest rejoice at every step in the Lord thy God. He has left thee a sweet hymn upon the subject, with which the weary travelers to Zion have oft refreshed their spirits. Take it up, and sing it after them. Study it; mix faith with it, and with perfect reliance on what God, who cannot lie, has promised in it to do for thee, sing and make melody with it in thy heart unto the Lord:

In that day sing ye unto her, A vineyard of red wine:
I the Lord do keep it; I will water it every moment;
Lest any hurt it, I will keep it night and day.
Fury is not in Me: who would set the briars and thorns against me in battle?
I would go through them; I would burn them together.
Or let him take hold of My strength, that he may make peace with Me;
And he shall make peace with Me. He shall cause them that come of Jacob to take root: Israel shall blossom and bud, and fill the face of the world with fruit.

O my good God and faithful keeper, I do believe these precious promises; help mine unbelief. Forgive my distrusting Thy faithfulness, and enable me steadfastly to rely upon it for the future. What return can

I make unto Thee for grafting me into the true vine? O Lord, this love surpasseth knowledge. I was fit for nothing but the fire, and Thou hast brought me into the vineyard of red wine, and hast enabled me to trust in that blood of the Lamb which cheereth God and man. On this my soul lives, and is refreshed; and being through grace in Him, and living upon Him, I bless Thee, holy Father, for Thy faithful promise to keep me unto the end. I am still an easy prey to all those who seek the hurt of my soul, but Thou hast given me Thy word that, lest any hurt me, Thou wilt keep me night and day.

I confess, gracious God, that I have dishonoured thee by doubting of thy love, and by questioning its unchangeableness, but now I believe that fury is not in Thee to any one branch in the true Vine. There is love, and nothing but love, in all Thy dealings with Christ, and with His. Forgive my guilty fears and suspicions of Thy forsaking me, arising from my weakness, and from the strength of mine enemies. I now see that Thou canst as easily consume them as fire can briars and thorns. Lord, increase my faith in Thy promised strength, that I may lay hold of it for peace, and may keep fast hold of it for maintaining peace with Thee, always and by all means. O grant me this, my good God, that my faith may work more by love. Let me take deeper root in Jesus, and grow up more into Him, blossoming and budding and flourishing in His vineyard. I depend upon Thee to keep me a branch in Him, and to make me a fruitful branch bringing forth plentifully the fruits of righteousness, which are by Christ Jesus to the glory and praise of God. I believe the work is Thine; Thou hast begun it, and Thou wilt carry it on until the day of the Lord Jesus. Thou art faithful to Thy Word and work. In dependence upon Thy faithfulness I hope to persevere. Let it be done unto me according to Thy promises, wherein Thou hast caused me to put my trust.

Hear, Lord, and answer for Thy mercies' sake in Jesus, to Whom, with Thee and the Eternal Spirit, three Persons in one Godhead, be equal glory and praise, for ever and ever. Amen.

We cannot come amiss to him that hath assurance. God is his. Hath he lost a friend? His Father lives Hath he lost an only child? God hath given him His only Son. Hath he scarcity of bread? God hath given him the finest of the wheat, the bread of life. Are his comforts, gone? He hath a Comforter. Doth he meet with storms? He knows where to put in for harbor. God is his Portion, and heaven is his haven. - *Thomas Watson*

Learn to know Christ and Him crucified. Learn to sing to Him, and say, "Lord Jesus, You are my righteousness, I am Your sin. You have taken upon Yourself what is mine and given me what is Yours. You have become what You were not so that I might become what I was not."
- *Martin Luther*

The greatest thing that we can desire, next to the glory of God, is our own salvation; and the sweetest thing we can desire is the assurance of our salvation. In this life we cannot get higher than to be assured of that which in the next life is to be enjoyed. All saints shall enjoy a heaven when they leave this earth; some saints enjoy a heaven while they are here on earth. - *Joseph Caryl*

Assurance will assist us in all duties; it will arm us against all temptations; it will answer all objections; it will sustain us in all conditions.
- *Edward Reynolds*

Assurance and comforts are desirable, but fruitfulness is absolutely necessary. The end why the Lord offers us comfort and assurance of His love, is to make us cheerful in His service, and to encourage us in His work, and engage our hearts in it thoroughly. - *David Clarkson*

DAY 10

THE NATURE AND BASIS OF ASSURANCE
BY A.W. PINK

AT THE COMMENCEMENT of Matthew 5 we find the Lord Jesus pronouncing blessed a certain class of people. They are not named as "believers" or saints," but instead are described by their characters; and it is only by comparing ourselves and others with the description that the Lord Jesus there gave, that we are enabled to identify such. First, He said,

"Blessed are the poor in spirit." To be "poor in spirit" is to have a feeling sense that in me, that is, in my flesh, "there dwelleth no good thing" (Rom. 7:18). It is the realization that I am utterly destitute of anything and everything which could commend me favorably to God's notice. It is to recognize that I am a spiritual bankrupt. It is the consciousness, even now (not years ago, when I was first awakened), that I am without strength and wisdom, and that I am a helpless creature, completely dependent upon the grace and mercy of God. To be "poor in spirit" is the opposite of Laodiceanism, which consists of self-complacency and self-sufficiency, imagining I am "rich, and in need of nothing."

"Blessed are they that mourn." It is one thing to believe the theory that I am spiritually a poverty-stricken pauper, it is quite another to have an acute sense of it in my soul. Where the latter exists, there are deep exercises of heart, which evoke the bitter cry, "my leanness, my leanness, woe unto me!" (Isa. 24:16). There is deep anguish that there is so little growth in grace, so little fruit to God's glory, such a wretched return made for His abounding goodness unto me. This is accompanied by an ever-deepening discovery of the depths of corruption which is still within me. The soul finds that when it would do good, evil is present with him (Rom. 7:21). It is grieved by the motions of unbelief, the swellings of pride, the surging of rebellion against God. Instead of peace, there is war within; instead of realizing his holy aspirations, the blessed one is daily defeated; until the stricken heart cries out, "O wretched man that I am! who shall deliver me from the body of this death?" (Rom. 7:24).

"Blessed are the meek." Meekness is yieldedness. It is the opposite of self-will. Meekness is pliability and meltedness of heart, which makes me submissive and responsive to God's will. Now observe, dear reader, these first three marks of the "blessed" consist not in outward actions, but of inward graces; not in showy deeds, but in states of soul. Note too that they are far from being characteristics which will render their possessor pleasing and popular to the world. He who feels himself to be a spiritual pauper will not be welcomed by the wealthy Laodiceans. He who daily mourns for his leanness, his barrenness, his sinfulness, will not be courted by the self-righteous. He who is truly meek will not be sought after by the self-assertive. No, he will be scorned by the Pharisees and looked upon with contempt by those who boast they are "out of Romans 7 and living in Romans 8." These lovely graces, which are of great price in the sight of God, are despised by the bloated professors of the day...

He who is really honest with himself and has had his eyes opened in some degree to see the awful sinfulness of self, and who is becoming more and more acquainted with that sink of iniquity, that mass of corruption which still indwells him, often feels that sin more completely rules him now than ever it did before.

- When he longs to trust God with all his heart, unbelief seems to paralyze him.

- When he wishes to be completely surrendered to God's blessed will, murmurings and rebellion surge within him.

- When he would spend an hour in meditating on the things of God, evil imaginations harass him.

- When he desires to be more humble, pride seeks to fill him.

- When he would pray, his mind wanders.

The more he fights against these sins, the further off victory seems to be. To him it appears that sin is very much the master of him, and Satan tells him that his profession is vain. What shall we say to such a dear soul who is deeply exercised over this problem? Two things:

FIRST: the very fact that you are conscious of these sins and are so much concerned over your failure to overcome them, is a healthy sign. It is the blind who cannot see; it is the dead who feel not - true alike naturally and spiritually. Only they who have been quickened into newness of life are capable of real sorrow for sin. Moreover, such experiences as we have mentioned above evidence a spiritual growth: a growth in the knowledge of self. As the wise man tells us, "he that increaseth knowledge increaseth sorrow" (Eccl. 1:18). In God's light we see light (Ps. 36:9). The more the Holy Spirit reveals to me the high claims of God's holiness, the more I discover how far short I come of meeting them. Let the midday sunshine into a darkened room, and dust and dirt which before were invisible are now plainly seen. So with the Christian: the more the light of God enters his heart, the more he discovers the spiritual filth which dwells there. Beloved brother, or sister, it is not that you are becoming more sinful, but that God is now giving you a clearer and fuller sight of your sinfulness. Praise Him for it, for the eyes of the vast majority of your fellows (religionists included) are blind, and cannot see what so distresses you!

SECOND: side by side with sin in your heart is grace. There is a new and holy nature within the Christian as well as the old and unholy one. Grace is active within you, as well as sin. The new nature is influencing your conduct as well as the old. Why is it that you so desire to be conformed to the image of Christ, to trust Him fully, love Him fervently, and serve Him diligently? These longings proceed not from the flesh. No, my distressed brother or sister, sin is not your complete master; if it were, all aspirations, prayers, and strivings after holiness would be banished from your heart. There are "as it were the company of two armies" (Song of Sol. 6:13) fighting to gain control of the Christian. As it was with our mother Rebekah, "the children struggled together within her" (Gen. 25:22) so it is with us. But the very "struggle" shows that the issue is not yet decided: had sin conquered, the soul would no longer be able to resist. The conqueror disarms his enemy so that he can no longer fight back. The very fact that you are still "fighting" proves that sin has not vanquished you! It may seem to you that it soon will: but the issue is not in doubt, Christ will yet save you from the very presence of sin.

In considering the basis of the Christian's assurance we must distinguish sharply between the ground of his acceptance before God, and his own knowledge that he is accepted by Him. Nothing but the righteousness of Christ-wrought out by Him in His virtuous life and vicarious death can give any sinner a perfect legal standing before the thrice holy God. And nothing but the communication of a new nature, a supernatural work of grace within, can furnish proof that the righteousness of Christ has been placed to my account. Whom God legally saves, he experimentally saves; whom He justifies, them He also sanctifies. Where the righteousness of Christ is imputed to an individual, a principle of holiness is imparted to him; the former can only be ascertained by the latter. It is impossible to obtain a scriptural knowledge that the merits of Christ's finished work are reckoned to my account, except by proving that the efficacy of the Holy Spirit's work is evident in my soul.

Once enrolled in the lists of this Church, sinners are safe for eternity; they are never cast away. The election of God the Father, the continual intercession of God the Son, the daily renewing and sanctifying power of God the Holy Ghost, surround and fence them in like a garden enclosed. Not one bone of Christ's mystical Body shall ever be broken; not one lamb of Christ's flock shall ever be plucked out of His hand. -
J.C. Ryle

Faith will make us walk, but assurance will make us run: we shall never think we can do enough for God. Assurance will be as wings to the bird, as weights to the clock, to set all the wheels of obedience running.
- *Thomas Watson*

None have assurance at all times. As in a walk that is shaded with trees and chequered with light and shadow, some tracks and paths in it are dark and others are sunshine. Such is usually the life of the most assured Christian. - *Ezekiel Hopkins*

Does assurance remain when comforts are gone? Take heed thou thinkest not grace decays because thy comfort withdraws…. Did ever faith triumph more in our Saviour crying "My God, my God!" Here faith was at its meridian when it was midnight in respect of joy.
- *William Gurnall*

A man's assurance may be as good, as true, when he lies on the earth with a sense of sin, as when he is carried up to the third heaven with a sense of love and foretaste of glory. - *John Owen*

DAY 11

ASSURANCE OF GRACE AND SALVATION
BY WILLIAM S. PLUMER

THE GENERAL IDEA running through the word assurance in the New Testament, is that of persuasion. He who is assured is persuaded. At least once assurance means belief, or ground of belief, as in Acts 17:31, where the Greek word is the same we commonly render faith. But when the New Testament speaks of assurance in the sense already explained, it uses a peculiar word (plerophoria) properly rendered full assurance, or much assurance. The four places where it occurs are Col. 2:2; 1 Thess. 1:5; Heb. 6:11; 10:22. The kindred verb is used in Luke 1:1, where it is rendered as most surely believed; in Rom. 4:21, where it is rendered being fully persuaded; and in Rom. 14:5, let every man be fully persuaded in his own mind. Some have defined assurance to be a firm persuasion of the certainty of anything, or a certain expectation of something future. Its general import is that of entire confidence, firm expectation, certain persuasion. In this discussion it is used in the sense of **full confidence of one's interest in Christ ending in final salvation**.

A. Some have asserted that assurance is of the essence of faith; that whoever has true faith knows and feels that he has it, and is certain that it is the faith demanded by God's word. It must be admitted that from the sixteenth century to the present there have been writers who used rash language on this subject. But let us note a few things:

1. When many of these men wrote they were combating a dangerous idea very prevalent in their day, namely, that a true faith might be wholly inoperative, inspiring no solid and lively hopes, and producing no change in men's lives. The error which they opposed was common, dangerous, and, if persisted in, fatal. They warred against a dead faith, and we must admit that there can be no more dangerous state than to settle down in a faith which produces no saving or powerful change in time, and inspires no good hopes for eternity.

2. Some have not sufficiently admitted that, as in other Christian graces, so in true faith there are degrees. The Word of God clearly admits that all the graces, faith in particular, may be very weak, even when genuine. So that we have the very phrase, *weak in faith*, with instructions how such shall be treated. Because of the feebleness of their believing, the disciples prayed, "Lord, increase our faith." Feeble faith may be as genuine as strong faith, though it administers comparatively little comfort in the day of

trial; yet such "shall be held up, for God is able to make him stand" (Rom. 14:4). In Scripture we have also the phrase strong in faith.

3. It is not safe to deny that any man can have an exercise of mind or heart without being conscious of all that passes within him; but that is very different from knowing that such an exercise of the soul is true faith. All our exercises of soul are to be tested and proved by God's word. True faith purifies the heart, works by love, overcomes the world, and quenches the fiery darts of Satan. Time and self-examination by God's word must show what is the true nature of all fair appearances in religion. Besides, there is surely a great difference between a persuasion that Jesus Christ is the only and sufficient Savior of lost men; and believing that we are savingly interested in His righteousness and intercession.

4. On a careful examination of all that is said by those who teach that assurance is included in the very essence of faith, it is apparent that many of them confound reliance with assurance. It is certainly true that no man believes a promise of God if he does not rely on it, and that no man believes in Jesus unless he looks to Jesus, leans upon Him, and relies on Him. Reliance is therefore of the essence of faith; and if by assurance is meant no more than reliance, there is no error taught, albeit there is a very unhappy use of terms.

Still it cannot safely be denied that some have pertinaciously taken the ground that no man had true faith without assurance of a saving interest in Christ.

B. Another error maintains the opposite extreme, and asserts that assurance of our personal interest in Christ is not attainable, and that a claim to it is mere presumption. Now let it be said:

1. Perhaps those who have taken this ground have been led to do so by noticing that a certain class of vain pretenders, who give no evidence of being regenerate, and who have none of the fruits of the Spirit, make a boast of their confident expectation of eternal life. There are some under this strong and strange delusion to such an extent that it will stick to them to the last. Even at the judgment day they will hug their delusions, and plead them before the face of the Son of God (Matt. 7:22-23).

2. Then some have, perhaps, stated the doctrine of assurance in a loose or harsh way, as if a wicked life could not disprove any such profession, or as if known or allowed sin ought not to shake all confident expectations of eternal happiness.

3.   All sober writers, who maintain the truth on this subject, agree that there are degrees of assurance, some being sufficient to produce calmness, others a high degree of boldness, and others leading to a triumphant defiance of all fears and foes, and to a joyful expectation of all good.

But it is neither safe nor scriptural to maintain that one cannot be on good and scriptural grounds assured of an interest in Christ, and of life eternal consequent thereon. The way is now open to say, that none but ignorant or carnal people will say that there is;

- No man who is grounded and settled in the truth of the Christian religion, in the divine inspiration and canonical authority of holy scripture;

- No man who walks by faith and not by sight;

- No man who has proven every doctrine he holds, and can give with meekness and fear a reason of the hope that is in him;

- No man who can say that the life he now lives, he lives by the faith of the Son of God;

- No man who can truly, modestly and unswervingly say that the Lord Christ is precious to his soul;

- No man who does constantly renounce all self-righteousness as filthy rags, and esteem himself the least of all saints;

- No one who can safely say, Lord, You know all things, You know that I love You;

- No one who does heartily and joyfully take the Lord Jesus Christ as his sole Mediator, his only Prophet, Priest, and King, as all his desire and all his salvation;

- No one who does truly and habitually say, I shall be satisfied when I awake with Your likeness, and until then I shall never rest contented with my state;

- No one who can say, I have a hearty respect to all God's commandments, and I do hate all sin in myself and others, but especially in myself; I do repent and humble myself for all my known sins; yes, I do abhor myself, and repent in dust and ashes, as I often have clear discoveries of the glory of God, especially in the person of Christ;

- No one who can truly say, I had rather be a doorkeeper in the house of my God than to dwell in the tents of wickedness;

- No one who habitually and prevailingly loves the light and comes to the light, both to find the path of duty and to detect his own secret faults;

- No one who hungers and thirsts after holiness more than he longs for necessary food and drink, and who is willing and ready at all times to crucify the flesh, with the affections and lusts;

- No one who is in the fear of the Lord all the day long, who lives as seeing Him who is invisible;

- No one who has a just and abiding sense of the vanity of all earthly things, of the shortness of time and, of the nearness and solemnity of eternity;

- No one who can be calm and quiet in God when all the world is in an uproar;

- No one who delights himself in God's being, name, perfections, government and glory;

- No one who, in the depth of his trials, says, Your will, O God, not mine, be done;

- No one who can say, This is my rejoicing, the testimony of my conscience, that in simplicity and Godly sincerity, not with fleshly wisdom, but by the grace of God, I have my conversation in the world;

- No one who gives all diligence to make his calling and election sure;

- No one who is clothed with humility, and abhors pride and all its hateful ways;

- No one who is vigilant day and night, never trusting in his own wisdom or strength, but habitually looking to the Most High for light and might;

- No one who has made up his mind to follow Christ even unto death, and not count his life dear if he may but win Christ and be found in Him;

- No one, who can either explain sufficiently to his own satisfaction the dark dispensations of God's providence, or with adoring reverence say what I know not now, I shall know hereafter;

- No one whose character is well proportioned, especially leading him to trust in God alone for every victory;

- No one who is so intent on doing and suffering the will of God that he is more anxious to know what will please God than what will please himself and all his fellow men;

- No one who blames himself more for wronging his fellow man than he blames another for injuring him, and who absolutely refuses to carry in his own bosom a grudge against any mortal;

- No one who so fears God as to be able habitually to maintain a control over his thoughts, affections, words, and actions;

- No one who is delighted with conversation and discourses which abase him in the dust and exalt his Redeemer, and lift his own thoughts to God's right hand, where are pleasures forever more;

- No one who loves his neighbor as himself, is fruitful in devices of usefulness, and counts that day lost on which he has done nothing for human virtue and happiness;

- No one who loves God's people with a love so tender and constraining that all who know him see that he is a lover of godly men;

- No one whose word is as good as his bond or his oath, and who says what he means, and means what he says;

- No one who is peaceable, gentle, easy to be entreated, and is full of kindness, even to slanderers and persecutors;

- No one who is unblameably observant of relative duties as husband, parent, child, subject, citizen, magistrate.

Can any sober, honest person say that such people cannot be found on earth? Well, if they can be found here, why should they not attain the assurance of grace and salvation? Does any say that while there are some such professors of religion on earth, yet the number of such is not large? In reply, it may be said, with sorrow, that there are not very many consistent, devoted, thorough-going followers of the Lamb. But the greater is the pity, and the greater is the shame. But let us go to the highest authority.

The word of God speaks of full **assurance of understanding**. The language is very strong: "That their hearts might be comforted, being knit together in love, and unto all riches of the full assurance of understanding, to the acknowledgment of the mystery of God, and of the Father, and of Christ, in whom are hid all the treasures of wisdom and knowledge" (Col. 2:2-3). The word rendered understanding in this place is so translated in every verse where it is found in the New Testament. Assurance of understanding supposes that intellectual doubts of the truth of the Bible, and of the system of doctrine really taught in the Scriptures, are all gone; and that if any difficulties on any branch of revealed truth remain, they are not such as to weaken confidence in the word of God; and the godly man is willing to give God His own time to make plain either hard texts or dark providences, not doubting that the Lord can easily do so at the right time.

Then the Scripture speaks of the full **assurance of faith**: "Let us draw near with a true heart, in full assurance of faith, having our hearts sprinkled from an evil conscience, and our bodies washed with pure water" (Heb. 10:22). This assurance does not chiefly relate to one's personal interest in Christ, but rather to the undoubted veracity of God in all He has spoken, particularly in the unerring truth of all He has told us in His word respecting the scheme of salvation, and a hearty and cordial reliance upon Christ as thus revealed. This assurance has every needed basis. It is most reasonable firmly to believe all God has said. It is a great dishonor to God when we lack a "thorough conviction of the truth of what is revealed in Scripture," or entertain "a cherished disposition to doubt or question the doctrines of the gospel." "The faithfulness of God is above all faithfulness." To question it is a sin. We ought steadfastly to believe everything God has made known to us. We ought to come to Him in full assurance of faith.

Then we have the full **assurance of hope**. Paul says, "And we desire that every one of you do show the same diligence to the full assurance of hope unto the end. That you be not slothful, but followers of those who through faith and patience inherit the promises" (Heb. 6:11-12). The Scriptures say much of hope. "We rejoice in hope of the glory of God;" "Hope makes not ashamed." "We are saved by hope." "You are called in one hope of your calling." "Be not moved away from the hope of the gospel." "Take for a helmet the hope of salvation" (Rom. 5:2, 5; 8:24; Eph. 4:4; Col. 1:23; 1 Thess. 5:8). These are mere samples of what abounds in the word of God. Though faith is always accompanied by hope, yet they are not the same. "Faith is the substance of things hoped for." The Syriac reads, "Faith is the persuasion of things in hope." That is, faith gives to things hoped for a present subsistence in the soul. "Faith credits the promises, hope looks to the things promised, and expects them. . . . Faith, eyeing the power and veracity of God, gives credit to the promises; hope, viewing them as not actually accomplished, desires them, delights in them, longs for their fulfillment, and expects it in faith." Another judicious writer says, "Faith is the credit we give to the truth of what is testified or promised in the gospel, and is founded on the veracity and faithfulness of God. The hope which attends this faith is a mixture of desire and joy, and an anticipation of enjoyment."

In the order of nature, assurance of understanding precedes assurance of faith, and both of these precede assurance of hope. When we have all three, we are happy indeed, and can defy all the assaults of fear and temptation.

But there are other forms of speech found in the word of God, which show that some of God's people, under every dispensation, have attained assurance. Thus, among the patriarchs, Enoch walked with God, and was not; for he "was translated, that he should not see death; and was not found, because God had translated him; for before his translation he had this testimony, that he pleased God" (Heb. 11:5). His translation was a great event; but it was preceded by a satisfactory and full persuasion, founded on good testimony, that he pleased God. The testimony was to himself, and preceded his translation. Then, too, another patriarch, the man of Uz, in the midst of as dark providences as ever surrounded a mere man, still held fast his confidence in the Son of God, saying "I know that my Redeemer lives" (Job 19:25). Not only was he confident that there was a Redeemer to others, but he was sure that that Redeemer was his Redeemer, and should accomplish all He had led His people to expect; and not merely that this great person should at some future time *live*, but that He was then *living;* as Jesus said, "Before Abraham was, I am." Here, then, under the patriarchal dispensation, we have two clear cases of full assurance.

Under the Mosaic dispensation David often expresses his assurance. Over and over again he says, "O Lord, truly I am Your servant; I am Your servant" (Ps. 116:16; 119:125; 143:12). In other terms no less confident does he declare the same thing in the twenty-third, the seventy-first, and the eighty-ninth Psalms, thus: "The Lord is my Shepherd; I shall not want." "In You, O Lord, do I put my trust." "I will sing of the mercies of the Lord forever" and many like phrases. Even poor Asaph, a man of a sorrowful spirit, and sometimes sunk in despondency and perplexity, did sometimes rise to the heights of a sublime assurance. Hear him: "You shall guide me with Your counsel, and afterward receive me to glory. Whom have I in heaven but You? and there is none upon earth that I desire beside You. My flesh and my heart fails; but God is the strength of my heart, and my portion forever." One can hardly find a more solemn or joyful declaration of blessed assurance than this. All this is in accordance with that glorious truth taught us by the evangelical prophet: "The work of righteousness shall be peace; and the effect of righteousness, quietness and assurance forever" (Isa. 32:17).

Under the gospel dispensation we have abundant proofs that assurance is attainable. Thus, poor Peter, though he had not long before behaved very badly, yet, having bitterly repented of his sad fall, said to the Searcher of Hearts, the Son of God Himself: "Lord, You know all things; You know that I love You" (John 21:17). In his last epistle, written shortly before his death, he says much of assurance, and tells Christians how they may attain unto it. In like manner blessed Paul, in his very last epistle, professes his assurance:

I know whom I have believed; and am persuaded that He is able to keep that which I have committed to Him against that day... I have fought a good fight, I have finished my course, I have kept the faith; henceforth there is laid up for me a crown of righteousness, which the Lord, the righteous Judge, shall give me at that day.
- 2 Tim. 1:12; 4:7-8

From other things said by Paul and by the beloved John, it seems clear that assurance was a common attainment in the primitive Church. (See Rom. 8:14-17, 35; 2 Cor. 5:1; Eph. 3:12; 1 John 3:14, 19; 4:13; 5:19). The reader can easily refer to these several passages, where strong confidence is expressed, the words we know frequently occurring. Nor can one examine with care the writings of the early Christians or of the Reformers without seeing that the confessors and martyrs of the early Church, and the heroes of the sixteenth century, did, to a large extent, attain to a blessed assurance.

Assurance is the fruit that grows out of the root of faith.
- *Stephen Charnock*

When we take the history of a child of God, compressed within the short period of a single day - mark what flaws, what imperfections, what fickleness, what dereliction in principle, what flaws in practice, what errors in judgment and what wanderings of heart make up that brief history - how we are led to thank God for the stability of the covenant, that covenant which provides for the full redemption of all believers, which from eternity secures the effectual calling, the perfect keeping and certain salvation of every chosen vessel of mercy! - *Octavius Winslow*

For we are not saved by believing in our own salvation, nor by believing anything whatsoever about ourselves. We are saved by what we believe about the Son of God and His righteousness. The gospel believed saves; not the believing in our own faith. - *Horatius Bonar*

If we be married to Christ, and He be jealous of us, depend upon it this jealous husband will let none touch His spouse. - *C.H. Spurgeon*

God… will not lightly or easily lose His people. He has provided well for us: blood to wash us in; a Priest to pray for us, that we may be made to persevere; and, in case we foully fall, an Advocate to plead our cause.
- *John Bunyan*

DAY 12

WESTMINSTER CONFESSION OF FAITH (1646)
Chapter 18: Of the Assurance of Grace and Salvation

ONE: Although hypocrites and other unregenerate men may vainly deceive themselves with false hopes and carnal presumptions of being in the favor of God, and estate of salvation (which hope of theirs shall perish): yet such as truly believe in the Lord Jesus, and love him in sincerity, endeavoring to walk in all good conscience before him, may, in this life, be certainly assured that they are in the state of grace, and may rejoice in the hope of the glory of God, which hope shall never make them ashamed.

TWO: This certainty is not a bare conjectural and probable persuasion grounded upon a fallible hope; but an infallible assurance of faith founded upon the divine truth of the promises of salvation, the inward evidence of those graces unto which these promises are made, the testimony of the Spirit of adoption witnessing with our spirits that we are the children of God, which Spirit is the earnest of our inheritance, whereby we are sealed to the day of redemption.

THREE: This infallible assurance doth not so belong to the essence of faith, but that a true believer may wait long, and conflict with many difficulties before he be partaker of it: yet, being enabled by the Spirit to know the things which are freely given him of God, he may, without extraordinary revelation, in the right use of ordinary means, attain thereunto. And therefore it is the duty of everyone to give all diligence to make his calling and election sure, that thereby his heart may be enlarged in peace and joy in the Holy Ghost, in love and thankfulness to God, and in strength and cheerfulness in the duties of obedience, the proper fruits of this assurance; so far is it from inclining men to looseness.

FOUR: True believers may have the assurance of their salvation divers ways shaken, diminished, and intermitted; as, by negligence in preserving of it, by falling into some special sin which woundeth the conscience and grieveth the Spirit; by some sudden or vehement temptation, by God's withdrawing the light of his countenance, and suffering even such as fear him to walk in darkness and to have no light: yet are they never utterly destitute of that seed of God, and life of faith, that love of Christ and the brethren, that sincerity of heart, and conscience of duty, out of which, by the operation of the Spirit, this assurance may, in due time, be revived; and by the which, in the meantime, they are supported from utter despair.

Sense of sin may be often great, and more felt than grace; yet not be more than grace. A man feels the ache of his finger more sensibly than the health of his whole body; yet he knows that the ache of a finger is nothing so much as the health of the whole body. - *Thomas Adams*

Great comforts do, indeed, bear witness to the truth of thy grace, but not to the degree of it; the weak child is oftener in the lap than the strong one. - *William Gurnall*

Assurance is not of the essence of a Christian. It is required to the bene esse (the well-being), to the comfortable and joyful being of a Christian, but it is not required to the esse, to the being of a Christian. A man may be a true believer, and yet would give all the world, were it in his power, to know that he is a believer. To have grace, and to be sure that we have grace, is glory upon the throne, it is heaven on this side of heaven.
- *Thomas Brooks*

I suppose many do not understand themselves, when they say they want assurance; for what better assurance would you have than the Word of God? If you have his Word, and take his Word, you need no better assurance. - *Ralph Erskine*

Grace with assurance is no less than heaven let down into the soul.
- *Bishop Hopkins*

DAY 13

NO SEPARATION FROM CHRIST JESUS
BY OCTAVIUS WINSLOW

DEATH CANNOT SEPARATE us from the love of God which is in Christ Jesus and all the blessings which that love bestows.

Death separate us? No! Death unites us the more closely to those blessings, by bringing us into their more full and permanent possession.

Death imparts a realization and a permanence to all the glorious and holy longings of the Christian. The happiest moment of his life is his last! Then it is that he feels how precious the privilege, and how great the eminence, of being a believer in Jesus.

And the day which darkens his eye to all earthly scenes opens it upon the untold, and unimaginable, and ever increasing glories of eternity! It is the birth day of his immortality! Then, Christian, do not fear death!

It cannot separate you from the Father's love. Nor can it, while it tears you from an earthly bosom, wrench you from Christ's. It may be that you shall have a brighter, sweeter manifestation of his love in death than you ever experienced in life.

Jesus, the Conqueror of death, will approach and place His almighty arms beneath you, and lay your head upon His loving bosom. Thus encircled and pillowed, you "shall not see death," but passing through its gloomy portal, shall only realize that you had actually died, from the consciousness of the joy and glory into which death had ushered you!

We have peace with God as soon as we believe, but not always with ourselves. The pardon may be past the prince's hand and seal, and yet not put into the prisoner's hand. - *William Gurnall*

It is natural to the soul to rest upon everything below Christ; to rest upon creatures, to rest upon graces, to rest upon duties, to rest upon divine manifestations, to rest upon celestial consolation, to rest upon gracious evidences, and to rest upon sweet assurances. Now the Lord, to cure His people of this weakness, and to bring them to live wholly and solely upon Jesus Christ, denies comfort, and denies assurance, etc., and for a time leaves His children of light to walk in darkness. Christians, this you are always to remember, that though the enjoyment of assurance makes most for your consolation, yet the living purely upon Christ in the absence of assurance, makes most for Christ's exaltation. He is happy that believes upon seeing, upon feeling, but thrice happy are those souls that believe when they do not see; that love when they do not know that they are beloved; and that in the want of all comfort and assurance, can live upon Christ as their only all. He that hath learned this holy art, cannot be miserable; he that is ignorant of this art cannot be happy.
- *Thomas Brooks*

That faith which is never assaulted with doubting is but a fancy. Assuredly that assurance which is ever secure is but a dream.
- *Robert Bolton*

Assurance is the fruit that grows out of the root of faith.
- *Stephen Charnock*

❖

There be many duties and dispositions that God requires which we cannot be in without assurance of salvation on good grounds. What is that? God bids us be thankful in all things. How can I know that, unless I know God is mine and Christ is mine? - *Richard Sibbes*

DAY 14

DOES PERSEVERANCE OF THE SAINTS PROMOTE IMPIETY AND FALSE ASSURANCE?
BY HERMAN WITSIUS

Being confident of this very thing, that he which hath begun a good work in you will perform it until the day of Jesus Christ - Philippians 1:6

OBJECTION:

Perseverance of the saints promotes impiety and false assurance.

ANSWER:

XLI. Hence appears the falsehood of the calumny of our adversaries, that, by this doctrine concerning the almighty conservation of God, a wide door is opened to profaneness and carnal security. That it is highly useful and effectual for the consolation of believers, provided it is true, will not be contradicted even by those who deny it. But nothing can be effectual for the consolation of the saints, which, at the same time, is not effectual for the promoting of holiness. For in every consolation, there is a demonstration of the beneficent love of God towards the wretched sinner who is solicitous about his salvation; and the clearer that demonstration of divine love is, and the more particular the application, the stronger also is the consolation. Besides, nothing is more powerful for inflaming our hearts with love to God, than the knowledge, sense, and taste of the divine love shed abroad in them. Whoever, therefore, most amplifies the powerful grace of God in his consolation, which impudence itself will not deny we do, presents to the saints the most powerful motives to divine love and the consequences thereof.

♦ **Perseverance of the Saints Promotes Piety.**

XLII. But let us more particularly show, that our doctrine is far more adapted to promote piety, than what our adversaries maintain concerning the unstable happiness of believers. And first, our doctrine doth certainly most of all illustrate the glory of God, which the opposite tends to obscure. We celebrate the infinite power of the Deity, whereby he can not only restrain our outward enemies from overthrowing our salvation, but also so fix the wavering disposition of our will, that it may not depart from the constant love of holiness; also his truth in the promises of the covenant of grace, on which we safely and securely rely; being assured, that he who hath promised will also perform; and his goodness, whereby he does not altogether reject or disinherit his children, or cut them off from the communion of Christ, even when they have fallen into some grievous sin, but by his fatherly chastisements, graciously recovers them from their fall and stirs them up to repentance; and his holiness, to which it is owing that he hides his face from his children, when, for some time, they seem to give too much way to sin, so that he does not grant them familiar access to himself, nor the influences of his consolations, but sharply stings and thoroughly terrifies their conscience with the sense of his indignation, lest he should appear to be like the sinner, or could bear with sin in his own people without resentment; and the efficacy of the merits and intercession of Christ, whereby he has acquired and preserves for himself an inheritance never to be alienated. In fine, we celebrate the invincible power of the Holy Spirit, who so preserves his mystical temple, that it neither can be destroyed, nor be made an habitation of impure spirits. But as the sum of our religion consists in glorifying God; so that which illustrates the glory of God in this manner, does most of all promote godliness.

◆ Arminianism is Injurious to God's Work of Salvation.

XLIII. But as the opposite doctrine separates the immutable bent of the free will to good from the efficacy of divine grace; as it maintains that God does not always perform what he has promised; as it will not grant that God's children, when they fall into some grievous sins, are chastised with rods, but disinherited and punished by spiritual death; as it asserts that the impetration of salvation by Christ may be perfect, and in every respect complete, though none should happen actually to be saved thereby, and that Christ was not always heard in his prayers; and that the Holy Spirit is sometimes constrained, by the mutability of the human will, to give up his habitation to the evil spirit; the opposite doctrine, I say, must in many respects, be injurious to the power, truth, and goodness of God the Father, to the merits and intercession of God the Son, and to the invincible efficacy of the Holy Spirit.

◆ Perseverance of the Saints Motivates Repentance.

XLIV. 2dly, Our doctrine is excellently adapted to allure the unconverted seriously to endeavour after conversion and repentance; for the more sure and stable that happens it, which is promised to the penitent, the more effectual is the motive taken from the consideration of it. The Scripture everywhere dissuades men from searching after the good things of this world, and encourages them to seek those good things which are spiritual, from this argument, that the former will perish, but the latter endure forever. John 6:27: "Labour not for the meat which perisheth, but for that meat which endureth unto everlasting life." 1 John 2:15, 17: "Love not the world: the world passeth away, and the lust thereof: but he that doeth the will of God abideth forever." And indeed, what can be more powerful to excite to repentance than this reflection? "As long as I am distracted with the anxious cares of this life, let my success be ever so great, I can only amass perishing treasures, of which I may perhaps be deprived in this very life, and the remembrance of which shall certainly torment me in the next. But if I diligently pursue the work of my conversion, I shall, from the very first moment of that, obtain that love of God in Christ, from which nothing shall ever be able to separate me again; and the sooner I enjoy that, the sooner I acquire that supreme good which is possessed without any danger of having my misery renewed."

♦ Arminianism Breeds Procrastination to Repentance.

XLV. But the opposite doctrine is adapted to procrastinate endeavours after repentance. For, when it is inculcated on a man, that a child of God by regeneration, after having for some time been engaged in the practice of holiness, not only may, but actually has often fallen away, and become a child of the devil, been disinherited by his heavenly Father, and is with greater difficulty renewed to repentance, the further progress he had made in holiness: the thought will easily be entertained by those who hear of exhortations to repentance, that there is no occasion to press the matter of their conversion so strenuously in their tender years, lest perhaps, considering the great inconstancy of unstable youth, they be overtaken by some great sin and their condition be far worse than it was before: that it is more advisable to wait for those years (for we generally promise ourselves long life), in which both our judgment is riper, and the mind usually pursues with more constancy what it has once applied to, enjoying in the meantime the delights of this world. Now, nothing can be more pestilential than this thought, which yet this doctrine suggests.

♦ Perseverance of the Saints Kindles Spiritual Steadfastness.

XLVI. 3dly, Our doctrine is also very powerful to confirm the elect, already converted in the spiritual life, and to quicken them to the constant practice of religion, which may be proved various ways: 1st, All the arguments which are raised from the possible apostasy of the saints, are taken from the fear of punishment and the terror of dreadful threatenings; but those taken from God's most powerful conservation, breathe nothing but his love and the incredible sweetness of divine grace. Moreover it is certain, that the children of God, "who have not received the spirit of bondage again to fear; but the spirit of adoption, whereby they cry, Abba, Father," Rom. 8:15, are more powerfully drawn by the cords of love, than driven by the scourge of terror; for, "that love of Christ constraineth us," 2 Cor. 5:14.

2dly, All our religion is nothing but gratitude; but it is clear, that that person more effectually promotes gratitude, who proves by cogent arguments, that the happiness bestowed from grace, shall be perpetual by the help of the same grace, than he who maintains, that though it be truly great, yet it may be lost.

3dly, It is equitable, that the better secured the reward of our duty is, the more diligent we should be in the practice of religion. For the consideration of the reward is among those things which render the commands of God sweet, Ps. 19:10. But we assure the faithful worshippers of God from his own word, that, from their very first entrance on the course of sincere godliness their reward is sure; calling upon them with the apostle, 1 Cor. 15:58: "Therefore, my beloved brethren, be ye stedfast, unmoveable, always abounding in the work, forasmuch as ye know that your labour is not in vain in the Lord." But our adversaries unhappily discourage all diligence, while they teach that we know not whether our labour shall be in vain or not, since it is possible we may fall away, and so have all along laboured for nothing.

Though no man merits assurance by his obedience, yet God usually crowns obedience with assurance. - *Thomas Brooks*

The gospel is the ground of the believer's assurance, while the Holy Spirit is its cause. - *J.C.P. Cockerton*

Assurance hath a narrow throat, and may be choked with a small sin. - *Thomas Fuller*

I think the first essential mark of the difference between true and false assurance is to be found in the fact that the true works humility. - *A.A. Hodge*

None have assurance at all times. As in a walk that is shaded with trees and chequered with light and shadow, some tracks and paths in it are dark and others are sunshine. Such is usually the life of the most assured Christian. - *Ezekiel Hopkins*

DAY 15

THE GOOD SHEPHERD
BY THOMAS WATSON

I am the good shepherd; I know My sheep. - John 10:14

CHRIST KNOWS ALL His sheep. His knowing His sheep is His loving them. This is a great consolation.

- **He knows every one of their names.** John 10:3, "He calls His own sheep by name."

- **He knows all the sighs and groans they make.** Psalm 38:9, "My groaning is not hidden from You."

- **He knows every tear they shed.** "I have seen your tears!" 2 Kings 20:5.

- **He bottles their tears as precious wine.** Psalm 56:8, "You keep track of all my sorrows. You have collected all my tears in Your bottle. You have recorded each one in Your book."

- **He knows all their sufferings.** "I have seen the way the Egyptians are oppressing them." Ex. 3:9. "The Lord saw the bitter suffering of everyone in Israel." 2 Kings 14:26

- **He knows all their good works**, all their works of piety and charity. "I know all the things you do. I have seen your hard work and your patient endurance." Revelation 2:2

"I am the good shepherd; I know My sheep." What a comfort is this!

He will place the sheep at His right hand and the goats at His left. Then the King will say to those on the right; Come, you who are blessed by My Father, inherit the Kingdom prepared for you from the foundation of the world! - Matthew 25:33-34

The Christian must trust in a withdrawing God. - *William Gurnall*

It is the very drift and design of the whole Scripture, to bring souls first to an acquaintance with Christ, and then to an acceptance of Christ, and then to build them in a sweet assurance of their actual interest in Christ. - *Thomas Brooks*

Some are afraid they have no faith at all, because they have not the highest degree of faith, which is full assurance, or because they want the comfort which others attain to, even joy unspeakable and full of glory. But for the rolling of this stone out of the way, we must remember there are several degrees of faith. It is possible thou mayest have faith, though not the highest degree of faith, and so joy in the Spirit. This is rather a point of faith than faith itself. It is indeed rather a living by sense than a living by faith, when we are cheered up with continual cordials. A stronger faith is required to live upon God without comfort, than when God shines in on our spirit with abundance of joy. - *Matthew Lawrence*

Now you will all be thus called one day to dispute for your souls, sooner or later; and therefore such skill you should endeavour to get in Christ's righteousness, how in its fullness and perfection it answereth to all your sinfulness. - *Thomas Goodwin*

The inward testimony of conscience, the sealing of the conscience, the sealing of the Spirit... far exceeds all the evidence of the senses. - *John Calvin*

IMPOSSIBLE FOR GOD TO LIE
BY THOMAS MANTON
PART 1

That by two immutable things, in which it was impossible for God to lie, we might have a strong consolation, who have fled for refuge to lay hold upon the hope set before us. - Hebrews 6:18

TO GIVE YOU THE OCCASION of these words, we must look back into the context. The apostle proveth the firmness of the promises, and yet the great need of faith and patience ere they be accomplished. He proveth both by the instance of Abraham, who was long exercised in waiting, and had God's promise ratified with the most solemn assurance that can be conceived under heaven, with an oath, which is held sacred and inviolable among all nations. But here some might object, that if Abraham had such a special assurance from God, what is that to us? To this the apostle replies, that though God's oath were given to Abraham, yet it concerns all the heirs of promise, every believer hath the same ground of certainty that Abraham had; so it is asserted, ver. 17, 'Wherein God, willing more abundantly to show unto the heirs of promise the immutability of his counsel, confirmed it by an oath.' There is an emphasis in the phrase, 'more abundantly.' God's oath was not given out of necessity, but out of condescension. Not out of necessity, as if his word was not valid and authentic without an oath, but he would give his oath that, over and above and by all solemn ways of assurance, the Lord would provide for our certainty and assurance, that we might have strong consolation upon solid grounds, 'That by two immutable things,' &c.

In the words we have the purport and the aim of God's oath, which is to give believers more solemn assurance. Take notice of three things:

♦ The **ground** of this assurance, 'That by two immutable things, in which it is impossible for God to lie.'

♦ The **fruit** of this assurance, 'That we might have strong consolation.'

♦ The **persons** to whom God hath given this assurance, we 'who have fled for refuge to lay hold of the hope that is set before us.'

Suitable to the three parts there are three main points:

1. God's word and oath are the immutable grounds of a believer's certainty and confidence.

2. That the fruit of this confidence and certainty is strong consolation.

3. That the persons to whom God hath deposited his oath, and by it administereth so strong a comfort and consolation, are those who fly for refuge to take hold of the hope that is set before them.

DOCT. 1: That God's word and God's oath are the immutable grounds of a believer's confidence and certainty; for these are the two immutable things spoken of. I shall speak of each distinctly.

First, God's single word is an immutable ground; having this, you have enough. And so it will appear if you consider the power and the certainty of it.

1. The power of God's word. His word is nothing else but the declaration of his powerful will; the force of it was discovered in creating the world. God created all things by his word: Ps. 33:9, 'He spake and it was done; he commanded, and it stood fast.' This whole fabric of heaven and earth, which we now behold with wonder, was made with a word. And mark, God's creating word and word of promise do not differ, they are both the word of God; and there is as much force and power in this word 'I will take away the heart of stone,' as there was in this word, 'Let there be light.' There is as much power in this sentence, 'I will make your vile bodies to be like to Christ's glorious body,' as there was in that word, 'Let there be a firmament.' God's word was powerful enough to make a world when it was nothing before. All the works of God subsist by the force of his word: Heb. 1:3, 'Upholding all things by the word of his power.' It is but for God to say, Let it continue, let it be, and either are accordingly. One word is enough to undo the world, and one word is enough to uphold and preserve it. God's word is the declaration of his almighty and powerful will; whatever he did in the world, he did it by his word. Therefore if you have this immutable ground, if God hath deposited and plighted his word, you have enough to establish strong consolation, for it is powerful to all purposes and intents whatsoever.

2. Consider the certainty of it. When the word is gone out of God's mouth, it shall not be recalled. The Lord prizeth his faithfulness above all things. The Scripture must be fulfilled whatever inconveniences come of it. Mark the whole course of providence, and you will find that God is very tender of his word; he valueth it above all his works: Luke 21:33, 'Heaven and earth shall pass away, but my words shall not pass away.' God is not so tender of heaven and earth but that he will break it all to pieces rather than not make good his word; though it be a curious frame and fabric, in which he hath displayed much of his glory, yet that shall be dissolved. Heaven and earth do only continue till all that is prophesied of in the word be fulfilled. We shall enjoy the comfort of his word in heaven, when all these things are melted away with a fervent heat. Nay, which is more, God valueth his word above the human life of Christ his

own Son. If God passed his word for it, his Son, who was the delight of his soul, equal to him in glory, must come from heaven, take a body, and suffer a cruel death: 'Lo, I come, in the volume of the book it is written of me, I delight to do thy will, O God,' Ps. 40:7. God had passed his word to the church that it should be so; therefore, rather than he would go back from his word, he sent Christ to die for a sinful world. There was no promise of more difficulty for God to grant nor for us to believe, than this of the incarnation and death of Christ; yet rather than go back from his word Christ must come and die an accursed and shameful death.

Secondly, The main thing is, what ground of consolation we have in God's oath. And there I shall (1.) Show the reasons why God gives us his oath over and above his word; (2.) The several advantages which we have by his oath in believing.

For the reasons why God should give this oath. An oath you know is given in matters doubtful. Philo saith, An oath is given for the manifestation of a matter which is secret and doubtful, and which cannot otherwise be determined. To swear in things apparent and matters clear is to take the name of God in vain. All matters which are clear are otherwise decided; matters of opinion, by argument; matters of fact, by testimony; matters of promise, by the single word of the party that promises, if he be a person of honour and credit; but always an oath supposes some doubt and controversy that cannot otherwise be determined. And so much the apostle intimates when he says, Heb. 6:16, 'It is the end of all strife' or controversy. Well, then, God's promises being of such absolute certainty, why doth the Lord deposit his oath with the creature, since his single and bare word is enough.

I answer: The matter itself needs it not, but only in regard of us. We look upon the promises with doubtful thoughts; there is a controversy between God and us; we have hard thoughts of God, as if he would not be so good as his word; therefore his oath is given, not to show the doubtfulness of the thing that is sworn, but the greatness of our unbelief. Austin saith, God hereby upbraids us with our unbelief, when he gives us an oath for the confirmation of any matter. Briefly, God's oath is given us for **two reasons**; to show us the certainty, and to show us the excellency of our privileges in Christ.

REASON 1:

To show us the certainty of our privileges in Christ. The world makes it a controversy and doubtful matter whether Christ came to die for sinners, yea or nay? whether God will save those that take sanctuary at Christ? God saith, Ay, and we say, No; and how shall the matter be decided? Observe it, and you will find that there are two things which we are apt to suspect in God; his good affection in making the promise, and his truth in keeping the promise. We suspect his good affection, especially when we are in pangs and gripes of conscience; and we suspect his truth in straits and difficulties, whenever in the course of God's providence we are cast into such a condition that we think he hath forgotten his promise.

Now the Lord might be highly offended with us for those wicked thoughts we entertain of his majesty, but in a gracious condescension he is pleased to put an end to the controversy by an oath. As if the Lord had said, Do you doubt of this? Will you put me to my oath? Here I am ready to take it; and that the matter may no longer remain in suspense, I swear by my life, by my holiness, by whatever you count sacred and excellent in me, that whoever among you, whatever he be, that is touched with a sense of his sin and misery by nature, if he will run to Christ for refuge, take sanctuary in Christ, if he doth belong to my unchangeable purposes of grace, I will surely without miscarrying bring him to a sure and eternal possession of glory; and for the present I will be a father to him, and guide him and keep him as the apple of mine eye; I will be his present help, his guardian, his counsellor, during the whole time of his abode in the world, where he is only liable to dangers.

This was the matter in controversy, and this is the substance of God's oath. And I shall show you how apt we are to distrust God in all this. We suspect, as I said, either his good affection in making the promise, or his truth in keeping the promise, so that we need this solemn way of assurance. Therefore; first, I shall speak to this, that we distrust his good affection, and will not believe God upon his single word. What should be the reason that nature is so abhorrent from this certainty and assurance, which so much concerneth our own peace and comfort?

TAKE SIX REASONS:

ONE: Partly because guilt is full of suspicion. We hate those whom we have wronged. First we hurt a person, then we hate him; so out of fear of revenge we suspect all that he doth, all acts of kindness, all tenders and offers of reconciliation which come from him. Let me exemplify it in men. Thus David speaks of his enemies: Ps. 120:7, 'I am for peace, but when I speak, they are for war.' David was the wronged party, and Doeg and Saul's courtiers had slandered him, and done him wrong. David was willing to forget all this injury, and he comes with an offer of peace, but all treaties of peace are in vain. This you will find to be the fashion of the world, when they have wronged a person, never to trust him anymore, lest they should give him opportunity of revenge. Thus do we deal with God; conscience knows we have wronged him, slighted his love, and put affronts upon his grace, and therefore, though he makes the first offer, we believe it not. Revengeful man cannot think God will be so gracious and merciful, therefore we cannot believe those ample purposes of reconciliation. It breaks the back of patience to think of forgiving seven times: 'Must I forgive seven times?' saith Peter. And therefore how can we believe the Lord will pardon so many thousand affronts we put upon him day by day? Thus we wrong God and sin away our faith, and therefore are not capable of so rich a comfort.

TWO: Partly because the way of salvation is so rare and wonderful, that a man can find no faith for it. The gospel is a mystery, so called by the apostle, 1 Tim. 3:16, 'Great is the mystery of godliness.' Nature affords no help here. Theology is natural, but not Christology. Nature believes there is a God, but not that there is a Christ. The sun and moon preach up a God, their sound is gone out into all lands, and proclaim everywhere that there is one infinite and eternal power; and conscience preacheth up a judge. But all these natural preachers are dumb and silent concerning Christ, not a word concerning a saviour and mediator. It could not enter into the thought of an angel to pitch upon such a remedy if God had not revealed it to them by the church: Eph. 3:10, 'To the intent that now unto the principalities and powers in heavenly places might be known by the church the manifold wisdom of God.' The angels did conceive of this great mystery by observing God's dispensations to the church. Well, then, the way of salvation being so rare and wonderful, we should never acquiesce and rest satisfied with bare declarations, but we need God's oath that the controversy may be determined. When an angel came to bring tidings of it to the Virgin Mary, though she were a holy woman, and had such an extraordinary way of assurance, yet you find her unbelief outstarts her obedience and submission to the will of God: 'How shall this be?' Luke 1:34. The incarnation of God, the conception of a virgin, the death of life itself, all these things are riddles and golden dreams to reason; and without a higher assurance than a bare word, we should not be easily satisfied.

THREE: Partly because the blessings and privileges we have in Christ are so great, and the persons which enjoy them so unworthy, as being nothing and deserving nothing, that they exceed all thought and belief: 1 Cor. 2:9, 'Eye hath not seen, nor ear heard, neither have entered into the heart of man, the things that God hath prepared for them that love him.' Mark, all the ways by which we can gain any knowledge of a thing, they come short; sense, fancy, reason, eye, ear, heart, of man cannot conceive and cannot tell what to make of these excellent privileges we have in Christ; they cannot furnish him with fit notions and apprehensions of such excellent glory as is revealed to us in him. To illustrate it by the creatures: If a man had been by when God made the world, as the angels were, if he had seen God laying the foundations of all things, he would have wondered what God was about to do, for what rare creature the Lord was about to frame this stupendous and wonderful fabric, arched with heaven, floored with earth, interlaced with waters, decked with fruits and plants, stored with creatures, and glazed, if I may so speak, with stars; who would ever have thought that all this furniture and provision was for man, a handful of dust, a poor worm not six feet long, that he might be lord of all things, vice-king and deputy under God?

Now, if a man would wonder at the honour and glory God put upon man at his creation, much more at the privileges of our redemption by Christ; they are matters to be wondered at indeed: 2 Thes. 1:10, 'Christ shall be glorified in his saints, and admired in all them that believe.' This place chiefly concerns the angels, when God puts such clarity and splendour upon the body that they shall wonder what Christ is about to do with such a contemptible creature as man, that newly came out of the grave of rottenness and dust. This text I am upon speaks of 'a hope set before us.' If this were but a little opened, as our ear hath received a little thereof, if we should tell you what preparation Christ hath made to bring the saints to glory, with what a glorious train of angels he will come from heaven, what mansions he hath prepared for us in his Father's house, and all this for those that have nothing and deserve nothing, unless it be extremity of misery; if a man should tell you Christ would come in such a state, and entertain the saints with such dearness of affection, and receive sinners into his bosom, that he would make them his fellow-judges, liken their bodies to his own glorious body for brightness and splendour, that such pieces of worms, and clods of earth shall be many times brighter than the sun, I tell you this would require a strong faith to believe it, and we had need of all the averment and assurance that can be given us under heaven. If an angel admires at the saints, certainly inferior creatures will suspect it. Alas! what a valuable price can we bring and pay to God for all this glory! We that judge all things by the laws of reason and commutative justice, for we give nothing but upon valuable consideration, what valuable price can we bring to God? What consideration can we give him for so great a glory, and how shall we think ever to be partakers of an estate so disproportionable to our merit and condition?

Therefore, because our privileges in Christ are so great and wonderful, we need not only God's word, but also his oath.

The Holy Spirit is no sceptic, and the things he has written in our hearts are not doubts or opinions, but assertions - surer and more certain than sense or life itself. - *Martin Luther*

None walk so evenly with God as they who are assured of the love of God. - *Thomas Manton*

Our assurance must be founded, built up and established on the mercy of God alone. - *Will Metzger*

Assurance... enables a child of God to feel that the great business of life is a settled business, the great debt a paid debt, the great disease a healed disease and the great work a finished work. - *J.C. Ryle*

When a man draws his comfort only from something that he finds within himself; from grace that he finds within, and not from grace without, then his comfort will not hold... Grace without is perpetual, that is to say, Christ's own personal obedience, in the merit of it, is perpetual. But the actings of grace within us are not perpetual, or not perpetually obvious to sight, and therefore cannot perpetually comfort... When therefore, you see the streams of a man's comfort run in this channel, when he draws all his comfort only or principally from... the actings of grace within, then you may say: Though the stream be now full, stay but a little, and ere long you will see it dried, and this man will be much discouraged.
- *William Bridge*

DAY 17

IMPOSSIBLE FOR GOD TO LIE
BY THOMAS MANTON
PART 2

FOUR: Partly because we ourselves are so false and fickle in all our contracts with one another, especially in our dealings with God, that we need to be bound with promise upon promise, and oath upon oath, and all little enough to restrain and hold us within the bounds of duty. Man is changeable, and breaks vows and covenants and promises, and snaps them asunder as a thread and tow is burnt asunder with fire, and will not be held with any obligation. It is a Greek proverb, Children play with nuts, and men with oaths. It is too often so. Perjury, though it be monstrous and barbarous, and dissolves the bonds of human societies and confederacies, yet it is no rare thing in the world, especially in the latter times. They are said among other sins to be infamous for covenant-breaking: 2 Tim. 3:3, 'Truce-breakers,' &c. Thus we deal with one another. But if we should be more faithful to men for the safety of our interest, yet how often do we break with God, and compass him about with lies: 2 Sam. 23:5, 'He hath made with me an everlasting covenant, ordered in all things, and sure.' We are false and fickle when God is sure. To-day we promise, to-morrow we fail. What vow did we ever make to God and kept it?

Now we are apt to judge of God's promises by our own. It is usual with man to transform God into his own likeness, and to muse of him as we use ourselves. The heathens did it grossly, and by a sensible picture; the apostle chargeth it upon them: Rom. 1:23, 'They changed the glory of God into an image made like to corruptible man.' They shaped God into the picture of man, and still according to the particular genius and fancy of each nation. The Spartans, being a warlike people, painted their gods in armour, suiting most with their disposition; the Ethiopians painted their gods black and their devils white, because they were a black people. But now we do it all spiritually: Ps. 50:23, 'Thou thoughtest I was altogether such an one as thyself.' We judge of God by ourselves, and draw a monstrous misshapen picture of him in our minds, as if he were revengeful, fierce, fallacious, fickle, and changeable as we are. Therefore, to meet with this sin doth the Lord so often disclaim the dispositions of a man, that we should not fancy him according to the lineaments of a man: Hosea 11:9, 'I will not execute the fierceness of mine anger, I will not return to destroy Ephraim; for I am God, and not man.' As if he had said, Do not measure me according to your model; I am not revengeful as you are, and changeable as you are; this is not my fashion. So Isa. 55:8, 9, 'For my thoughts are not your thoughts, neither are your ways my ways, saith the Lord. For as the heavens are higher than the earth, so are my ways higher than your ways, and my thoughts than your thoughts.' You see the distance between earth and heaven is so wondrous great that the earth cannot reach it with its mountains, cedars, turrets, smoke, and vapours; it is so great that a star of the heavens, as big as the earth, seems to be but a spangle: so infinitely more are the workings of my thoughts, and my heart different from your thoughts and your heart.

More particularly and suitable to the present case: Num. 23:19, 'God is not a man that he should lie, neither the son of man, that he should repent: hath he said, and shall he not do it? or hath he spoken it, and shall he not make it good?' Man is as unstable as water; his point varieth according to the different posture of the times and situation of his own interest and advantage; but it is not so with me, saith the Lord. Men say and do not, but God's Yea is always yea, and his No is always no. This was the speech of Balaam, who was called a false prophet, not from the matter of his prophecy, but only from his aims. But if you will have it from a more authentic hand, you have it out of the mouth of Samuel: 1 Sam. 15:29, 'The strength of Israel will not lie, nor repent; for he is not a man that he should repent.' Mark the reason, for he is not a man. To be a man and to be changeable is all one. Certainly the frequent inculcation of such passages in scripture showeth that we are apt to measure infiniteness by our own scantling and size. And therefore, this being man's natural thought, God in a condescension, and by way of check, is pleased to give the creature this assurance, we have his word and his oath; so that if we would but afford him the favour we use to show to an honest man, we have no ground of diffidence and distrust.

FIVE: Another cause of this unbelief is enmity to the gospel. There is a natural contrariety in our hearts both to the privileges and duties of the gospel, and because we hate it, we do not easily believe it. The pride of man's heart sets him against the privileges of the gospel, and carnal liberty against the obedience of it. Man is a proud creature, and would be self-sufficient; he is loath to be beholden to God, as a proud man loves a russet coat of his own better than a silken garment that is borrowed of another. Thus the apostle complains of the Jews: Rom. 10:3, 'They being ignorant of God's righteousness, and going about to establish a righteousness of their own, have not submitted themselves to the righteousness of God.' There needs some submission and bearing down of the pride of man, all is borrowed; here Christ is all, and doth all, he hath merited for all, and suffered for all. Now this suits not with the pride of man's heart, who would be sufficient to himself, and establish a personal merit in himself. And then especially is this pride betrayed when a man hath anything to trust to and rest in, as civil righteousness or a formal profession; it is a hard matter then to bring men to submit to the righteousness of God, to come hungry and thirsty for Christ's righteousness. There is no pride so deadly and mischievous, and opposite to the gospel, as the pride of self-conceit and self-sufficiency; yet this is natural to us; therefore God doth not only say, but swear, that we shall never enter into his rest unless we take this course, and run to this hope that is before us. And as pride opposeth the privileges of the gospel, so carnal liberty opposeth the obedience of the gospel. Men are loath to stoop and submit to God's terms. Christ is to be Lord as well as Saviour. Now the world will not hear of laws and restraints. You know the nations were all for casting away the bonds and cords: Ps. 2:3, 'Let us break their bonds asunder, and cast away their cords from us.' In the latter ages of the world, it is foretold in the prophecies of scripture, that the church is in danger of turning to libertinism: we cast away yoke after yoke, till we have left Christ nothing but an empty title. How busy are men now to find out a north-east-passage, a nearer cut to heaven; and therefore the Lord swears, and ratifies the whole tenor of the gospel by an oath, to meet with our enmity and natural contrariety, which makes us so apt to misbelieve.

SIX: Another cause why those that are touched with a sense of sin suspect God's good affection is a jealousy of assurance, or a secret fear of presuming. All the doubts and scruples of a troubled conscience come to this issue, and may all be referred to this head, a fear of presuming. Many will plead the number of their sins, and how many affronts they have put upon the grace of God. Some will plead the greatness and the aggravations of their sins, relapses into sin, sins against light, against the advantages of grace; but they all end in this one thing, a fear of being too bold with the comforts of the gospel, and that comfort doth not belong to persons in their case. This is the cable-rope which keeps them from floating out amain upon the ocean of God's mercy, as if the Lord delighted in their grief rather than in their assurance and satisfaction. Usually thus it is with disturbed consciences. Trouble that is once swallowed is hardly got up again; and men think sadness is more pleasing to God than comfort, and that doubts suit with a christian frame rather than confidence, and so they hug a distemper instead of a duty. Therefore the Lord is fain to swear that certain it is. Nay, it is not for nothing that this makes the heart of Christ so joyful, that we live upon the provision he hath made for us: John 15:11, 'These things have I spoken unto you, that my joy might remain in you, and that your joy might be full.' This is the very aim of God's oath; he would show, as I shall further clear by and by, that our assurance is more pleasing to him than our doubting; that he is better pleased with our comfort, nay, though it rise up to strong comfort, than with our sorrow. Thus you see that diffidence and incredulity is deeply rooted in our nature; yea, believers themselves are liable to many doubts, out of the relics of atheism and unbelief that yet remain in them.

Secondly, I am to show that we are apt to suspect his truth in keeping his promise. When straits and difficulties come, and things go cross to our expectation, we had need of more than God's single word. There is not one of an hundred that lives by faith, and can bottom his comfort on a single promise, and can rejoice in the Lord his God when outward supports fail. We are led altogether by sense, and therefore in cross providences we look upon promises as words of course, and are apt to say, Where are his promises, and the soundings of his bowels? and where is the ready help which God hath promised in the time of trouble? And therefore, as a prop to the soul, he hath backed his promise with an oath.

Mark it, Christians, it is very usual, even with God's dearest children, to unravel their hopes, and to question all upon a cross providence; as David: Ps. 116:11, 'I said in my haste, All men are liars.' Why doth David retract that charge, and impute it to his haste? The apostle saith, Rom. 3:4, 'Let God be true, and every man a liar.' We are changeable creatures, our beings are a lie; today we are, and to-morrow we are not; and so our promises are a lie; we say, and do not; and therefore why doth David impute it to his haste, as if he had spoken something that were untrue? Certainly, there was some blame in the expression, for he acknowledgeth it was spoken in haste. The speech hath respect to those messages and assurances which were brought to him from the mouth of God by Samuel, Nathan, and other prophets. They comforted him with God's promises, and now he was thunderstruck, blasted with some sore affliction, far enough from the case of a man that had many assurances from heaven; now 'all men are liars,' prophets and all. Once more, Ps. 31:22, 'I said in my haste, I am cut off from before thine eyes; nevertheless thou heardest the voice of my supplications, when I cried unto thee.' God hath cast off all care of David; he doth not look after a poor banished man, which wandereth up and down in the wilderness, a poor flea that is chased and hunted to and fro.

Such pets and passions of distrust, such irregular and unbelieving thoughts usually have we upon any cross providence, when sense contradicts the promise. Always we find sense and distrust making lies of God; therefore a single promise will not serve the turn, but we need an oath. Surely if God hath sworn, we may wait upon him. Doubts, now God hath passed his oath, do but accuse him of perjury. And therefore you shall see the oath of God hath always been the refuge of the saints even in the worst of times, when they seemed most of all to lour upon their hopes and expectations, Hab. 3:9. The affairs of the church were at that time desperate; but saith the prophet, 'Thy bow was made quite naked, according to the oaths of the tribes, even thy word. Selah.' God for his covenant and oath's sake revived the affairs of the church when they were at a desperate pass. It is there expressed in: the plural number, oaths, because they were often renewed with the church; and they are called 'the oaths of the tribes,' because this was the church's treasure, because of the oath God made with the tribes, for it is not meant of the oaths the church made with God. Look, as the covenant of Abraham is God's covenant made with Abraham, and the mercies of David were God's mercies bestowed upon David, so the oaths of the tribes are not taken actively for the oaths which the tribes deposited with God, but passively for the oath God deposited with the tribes, that is, the church. God took this bow out of the case, and bestows the arrows of his vengeance upon the adversaries of the church.

That this exposition is true, it appeareth in what follows, 'Even thy word. Selah.' There is his word, and that confirmed by an oath, the two immutable things; these relieve the sinking state of the church. It goes ill with the church a long time, that we might have experience what God can do. Look what Florus said of the state of Rome, "The Romans were often overcome in battle, but never in war." So of the church; they go by the worst in some particular cases, and in some particular times, that we might try God, and God may try us: but we are safe; God will remember the oaths of the tribes; the oath of God will relieve the most desperate case. It is rude blasphemy to say God will not make good his oath. Thus you see why God would deposit his oath.

REASON 2:
God sweareth, as for the confirmation of his grace in Christ, and to show the certainty of our privileges in Christ, so for the commendation and excellency of them. An oath is not lawful but in weighty matters; it must be taken in judgment, as well as in righteousness and truth, Jer. 4:2. In judgment, that is, considerately, upon weighty occasions. It is a profaning the name of God, and of such a solemn ordinance and part of worship, to make an oath to lacquey upon trifles, and upon every small matter; it must be in matters of weighty concernment.

There is a severe penalty and sanction annexed to the taking of God's name in vain, either rashly or falsely: 'The Lord will not hold him guiltless that taketh his name in vain.' So whatever is established by God's oath must needs be great and excellent. Certainly God would not swear but in weighty matters; therefore one of his aims was that we might the more regard our privileges in Christ. The apostle proveth the excellency of Christ's priesthood by the oath wherewith it was ratified: Heb. 7:20, 21, 'And inasmuch as not without an oath he was made priest; for those priests were made without an oath, but this with an oath by him that said unto him, The Lord sware, and will not repent,' &c. He alludes to Ps. 110:4, where God is brought in, saying to Christ, 'The Lord hath sworn, and will not repent, Thou art a priest for ever after the order of Melchisedeck.' Such administrations as are confirmed with an oath have upon them a seal and mark of special excellency. The Lord foresaw that as we were apt to disbelieve the gospel, so also to despise it; and therefore, to shame us for our neglect as well as our unbelief, to awaken our attention and quicken our speed and earnest pursuit, the Lord swears; his word should be regarded, much more his oath.

When we are busy about the world; and neglect the great salvation, we put a scorn upon God, as if the things he hath confirmed by oath were not worth the looking after. When we prefer worldly comforts as more certain, oh! what an injury is this to the oath of God! We read of the sure mercies of David, but you are all for lying vanities. We are naturally for the comforts that are before us, and look upon it as a riddle to grow rich in promises and to live by faith. Are uncertain riches more to be trusted, and a better refuge and sanctuary for your souls than God's oath? It is a sign you slight his confirmation and commendation, and so count him false and foolish in all the things he proposeth to you.

God forbid, say you, that we should be guilty of such a blasphemy. You do it not in word, but this is the necessary interpretation of your actions. If a man should offer you a good bargain upon very easy terms, that would bring you a thousand pounds profit, and should confirm it by oath, though you did not tell him that he did deceive you with words, yet if you go away never heeding it, but should run after smaller matters which you purchase with great hazard, would not this argue you counted him but false and foolish; or the thing not worth the taking and looking after? So when God hath pawned his oath, that his grace and immutable counsel for salvation belonged to you if you would but take sanctuary in Christ, do you not count him false and foolish in the proposal when you run after carnal satisfactions, which are purchased with the loss of your souls?

Assurance is the believer's ark where he sits, Noah-like, quiet and still in the midst of all distractions and destructions, commotions and confusions... [However] most Christians live between fears and hopes, and hang, as it were, between heaven and hell. Sometimes they hope that their state is good, at other times they fear that their state is bad: now they hope that all is well, and that it shall go well with them forever; [then] they fear that they shall perish by the hand of such a corruption, or by the prevalence of such or such a temptation... They are like a ship in a storm, tossed here and there. - *Thomas Brooks*

Assurance of hope is more than life. It is health, strength, power, vigour, activity, energy, manliness, and beauty. - *J.C. Ryle*

Christians should never rest until the soul evidences that it is the Lord's... While our interest in his favour is doubtful, what happiness can we enjoy? - *C.H. Simeon*

Our assurance is only as strong as our faith. - *R.C. Sproul*

Assurance is a jewel for worth but not for rarity. - *C.H. Spurgeon*

DAY 18

DEVOUR ME, DEVOUR ME!
BY THOMAS BROOKS

ASSURANCE WILL SWEETEN the thoughts of death and all the aches, pains, weaknesses, sicknesses, and diseases, which are the forerunners of death; yes, it will make a man look and long for death.

Nazianzen said to the king of terrors, "Devour me, devour me! Death cures all diseases, the aching head, and the unbelieving heart!" Assurance makes a man smile upon the king of terrors. The assured soul knows that death shall be the funeral of all his sins, all his sorrows, all his afflictions, all his temptations.

He knows that death shall be the resurrection of his joys. He knows that death is both an outlet and an inlet; an outlet to sin; and an inlet to the soul's clear, full, and constant enjoyment of God! And this makes the assured soul to sing it sweetly out, "O death, where is your sting? O grave, where is your victory? "I desire to depart and be with Christ, which is better by far!" "Make haste, my beloved." "Come, Lord Jesus, come quickly!"

Now death is more desirable than life. Now says the soul, "let him fear death, who is averse to go to Christ." The Persians had a certain day in the year, in which they used to kill all serpents and venomous creatures. The assured Christian knows that the day of death will be such a day to him; and that makes death lovely and desirable. He knows that sin was the midwife which brought death into the world; and that death shall be the grave to bury sin. And therefore death is not a terror, but a delight unto him.

He fears it not as an enemy but welcomes it as a friend.

Assurance of faith can never come by the works of the law. It is an evangelical virtue, and can only reach us in a gospel way. - *C.H. Spurgeon*

A letter may be written, when it is not sealed; so grace may be written in the heart, and the Spirit may not set the seal of assurance to it.
- *Thomas Watson*

When I sit alone, and can have a settled assurance of the state of my soul, and know that God is mine, I can laugh at all troubles and nothing can daunt me. - *Hugh Latimer*

Our hope is not hung upon such an untwisted thread as, "I imagine so," or "It is likely;" but the cable, the strong rope of our fastened anchor, is the oath and promise of Him who is eternal verity. Our salvation is fastened with God's own hand, and Christ's own strength, to the strong stake of God's unchangeable nature. - *Samuel Rutherford*

Assurance will make a man fervent, constant, and abundant in the work of the Lord. When the assured Christian hath done one work, he is calling out for another. What is next, Lord, says the assured soul: what is next? An assured Christian will put his hand to any work, he will put his neck in any yoke for Christ; he never thinks he hath done enough, he always thinks he hath done too little, and when he hath done all he can, he sits down, saying, I am an unprofitable servant. - *Thomas Brooks*

DAY 19

ALL THE HELL THAT YOU SHALL EVER HAVE!
BY THOMAS BROOKS

CONSIDER CHRISTIAN, that all your trials and troubles, calamities and miseries, crosses and losses, which you meet with in this world is all the hell that you shall ever have! Here and now you have your hell. Hereafter you shall have your heaven!

This is the worst of your condition; the best is yet to come!

Lazarus had his hell first, his heaven last; but Dives had his heaven first, and his hell at last.

- ◆ Here you have all your pangs, and pains, and throes that ever you shall have! Your ease, and rest, and pleasure is yet to come!
- ◆ Here you have all your bitters; your sweets are yet to come!
- ◆ Here you have your sorrows; your joys are yet to come!
- ◆ Here you have all your winter nights; your summer days are yet to come!
- ◆ Here you have your evil things; your good things are yet to come!

Death will put an end to all your sins and to all your sufferings! Death will be an inlet to those joys, delights, and comforts, which shall never have an end!

Who can seriously meditate upon this, and not be silent under God's most smarting rod?

The true assurance of salvation, which the Spirit of God hath wrought in any heart, hath that force to restrain a man from looseness of life, and to knit his heart in love and obedience to God, as nothing else hath in all the world. It is certainly either the want of faith and assurance of God's love, or a false and carnal assurance of it, that is the true cause of all the licentiousness that reigns in the world. - *Arthur Hildersham*

None walk so evenly with God as they who are assured of the love of God. Faith is the mother of obedience, and sureness of trust makes way for strictness of life. When men are loose from Christ, they are loose in point of duty, and their floating belief is soon discovered in their inconstancy and unevenness of walking. We do not with alacrity engage in that of the success of which we are doubtful: and therefore when we know not whether God will accept us or not, when we are off and on in point of trust, we are just so in the course of our lives, and serve God by fits and starts. It is the slander of the world to think assurance an idle doctrine. - *Thomas Manton*

None have assurance at all times. As in a walk that is shaded with trees and checkered with light and shadow, some tracks and paths in it are dark, and others are sunshine: such is usually the life of the most assured Christian. - *Bishop Hopkins*

A lazy Christian shall always want four things: viz., comfort, contentment, confidence, and assurance. God hath made a separation between joy and idleness, between assurance and laziness, and therefore it is impossible for thee to bring these together, that God hath put so far asunder.
- *Thomas Brooks*

If you have assurance of your justification, do not abuse it. It is abusing assurance when we grow more remiss in duty; as the musician, having money thrown him, leaves off playing. - *Thomas Watson*

DAY 20

A LETTER OF ASSURANCE
BY JOHN NEWTON

DEAR FRIEND,

I hope that you have found your trials so sweetened, and so sanctified, by God's blessing, that you have been enabled to rejoice in them! Whatever may be the immediate causes of your troubles, they are all under the direction of a gracious hand and each, in their place, cooperating to a gracious end. Your afflictions all come from God's heart, who loves you better than you love yourself! They are all tokens of His love and favor and are necessary means of promoting your growth in faith and grace. You are in the hands of Him who does all things well, and conducts His most afflictive dispensations to those who fear Him, with wisdom and mercy!

The Lord knows what is best for you! When there is an especial need-be for your being in the furnace, He knows how to support you; and at what season, and in what manner, deliverance will best comport with His glory and your good. These are the two great ends which He has in view, and which are inseparably connected together.

He knows our frame, and of what we are made. His pity exceeds that of the most tender parent. And though He causes grief, He will have compassion. Your afflictions which at present are not joyous but grievous, shall, when you have been duly exercised by them, yield the peaceable fruits of righteousness. I trust the Lord gives you a measure of patience and submission to His holy will. If so, everything shall be well, and when He has fully tried you, you shall come forth as gold!

The thoughts of what we have deserved at His hands, and what Jesus suffered for our sakes, when applied by his Holy Spirit, have a sovereign efficacy to compose our minds, and enable us to say, "Not my will but may Yours be done!" How unspeakably better is it to be chastened by the Lord now, than to be left to ourselves for a season, and at last condemned with the world.

The path of affliction is sanctified by the promises of God, and by the consideration of our Lord Jesus, who walked in it Himself, that we might not think it too much to tread in His steps. Yes, it has been a beaten path in all ages; for the innumerable multitudes of the redeemed who are now before the eternal throne, have entered the kingdom by no other way. Let us not then be weary and faint, but cheerfully consent to be the followers of those who, through faith and patience, are now inheriting the promises!

If, after much tribulation, we stand accepted before the Lord in His glory, we shall not then think much of the difficulties we met with in our pathway to glory. Then sorrow and sighing shall cease forever, and songs of triumph and everlasting joy shall take their place! Oh, happy transporting moment, when the Lord God Himself shall wipe every tear from our eyes! Until then, may the prospect of this glory which shall be revealed, cheer and comfort our hearts! Hitherto the Lord has helped us. He has delivered us in six troubles and we may trust Him in the seventh. Whatever storms may arise, we have an infallible and almighty Pilot, who will be a Sun and a Shield to those who love Him!

As long as we live, new trials will be needful. It is not that the Lord delights in grieving us and putting us to pain; on the contrary, He rejoices in the prosperity of His servants. No, it is not for His pleasure but for *our profit*, that we may be made partakers of His holiness!

Perhaps you may have observed a bird, in a hedge, or upon the boughs of a tree; if you disturb it, it will move a little higher and thus you may make it change its place three or four times. But if it finds, after a few trials, that you continue to follow it, it takes wing at last, and flies away! Thus it is with us! When the Lord drives us from one creature-rest, we immediately perch upon another! But He will not allow us to stay long upon any. At length, like the bird, we are sensible that we can have no safety, no stable peace below! Then our hearts take flight and soar heavenwards, and we are taught by His grace to place our treasure and affections out of the reach of earthly vanities. So far as this end is accomplished, we have reason to be thankful and say, *happy rod that brought me nearer to my God!*

To make sense and feeling the judges of our spiritual conditions, what is
it but to make ourselves happy and miserable, righteous and unrighteous,
saved and damned in one day, ay, in one hour.... What is this but to toss
the soul to and fro, and to expose it to a labyrinth of fears and scruples?
What is this but to cast a reproach upon Christ, to gratify Satan, and to
keep yourselves upon the rack? Well, doubting souls, the counsel that I
shall give you is this, be much in believing, and make only the Scripture
the judge of your condition; maintain the judgement of the Word against
the judgement of sense and feeling... If you resolve to make sense and
feeling the judge of your conditions, you must resolve to live in fears, and
lie down in tears. - *Thomas Brooks*

Motion is the most perfect discoverer of life. He that can stir his limbs, is
surely not dead. The feet of the soul are the affections. Hast thou not
found in thyself a hate and detestation of that sin whereinto thou hast
been miscarried? Hast thou not found in thyself a true grief of heart, for
thy wretched indisposition to all good things? Without a true life of
grace, these things could never have been. - *Joseph Hall*

Faith rests on the naked Word of God; that Word believed
gives full assurance. - *H.A. Ironside*

Sin can never quite bereave a saint of his jewel, his grace; but it may steal
away the key of the cabinet, his assurance. - *William Jenkyn*

The doctrine of assurance, biblically understood, keeps the
saint on his toes. - *J.A. Motyer*

DAY 21

THE COMPASSION OF CHRIST TO WEAK BELIEVERS
SAMUEL DAVIES
PART 1

A bruised reed shall He not break, and smoking flax shall He not quench.
- Matthew 12:20

THE LORD JESUS POSSESSES all those virtues in the highest perfection, which render him infinitely amiable, and qualify him for the administration of a just and gracious government over the world. The virtues of mortals, when carried to a high degree, very often run into those vices which have a kind of affinity to them. "Right, too rigid, hardens into wrong." Strict justice steels itself into excessive severity; and the 'man' is lost in the 'judge.' Goodness and mercy sometimes degenerate into softness and a sentimentalism, inconsistent with justice.

But in Jesus Christ these seemingly opposite virtues center and harmonize in the highest perfection, without running into extremes. Hence He is at once characterized as a Lamb, and as the Lion of the tribe of Judah: a lamb for gentleness towards humble penitents; and a lion to tear His enemies in pieces! Christ is said to judge and make war (Rev. 19:11); and yet he is called The Prince of Peace (Isaiah 9:6). He will at length show himself dreadful to the workers of iniquity; and the terrors of the Lord are a very proper topic whence to persuade men. But now He is patient towards all men, and He is all love and tenderness towards the vilest penitent.

The meekness and gentleness of Christ is to be my pleasing topic; and I enter upon it with a particular view to those mourning, desponding souls among us, whose weakness renders them in great need of strong consolation. To such, in particular, I address the words of my text, "A bruised reed shall He not break, and smoking flax shall he not quench." The general meaning of my text seems to be contained in this observation: That the Lord Jesus has the tenderest and most compassionate regard to the feeblest penitents, however oppressed and desponding; and that He will approve and cherish the least spark of true love towards himself.

A '**bruised reed**' seems naturally to represent a soul at once feeble in itself, and crushed with a burden; a soul both weak and oppressed. The reed is a slender, frail plant in itself, and therefore a very proper image to represent a soul that is feeble and weak.

A bruised reed is still more frail, hangs its head, and is unable to stand without some prop. And what can be a more lively emblem of a poor soul, not only weak in itself, but bowed down and broken under a load of sin and sorrow, that droops and sinks, and is unable to stand without divine support? Strength may bear up under a burden, or struggle with it, until it has thrown it off; but oppressed weakness, frailty under a burden; what can be more pitiable? and yet this is the case of many a poor penitent. He is weak in himself, and in the meantime crushed under a heavy weight of guilt and distress.

And what would become of such a frail oppressed creature, if, instead of raising him up and supporting him, Jesus should tread and crush him under the foot of his indignation? But though a reed, especially a bruised reed, is an insignificant thing, of little or no use, yet "a bruised reed he will not break," but he raises it up with a gentle hand, and enables it to stand, though weak in itself, and easily crushed to ruin.

Perhaps the imagery, when drawn at length, may be this: "The Lord Jesus is an Almighty Conqueror, marches in state through our world; and here and there a bruised reed lies in his way. But instead of disregarding it, or trampling it under foot, He takes care not to break it. He raises up the drooping straw, worthless as it is and supports it with his gentle hand." Thus, poor brokenhearted penitents, thus He takes care of you, and supports you, worthless as you are. Though you seem to lie in the way of His justice, and it might tread you with its heavy foot, yet He not only does not crush you, but takes you up, and inspires you with strength to bear your burden and flourish again.

Or perhaps the imagery may be derived from the practice of the ancient shepherds, who were accustomed to amuse themselves with the music of a pipe of reed or straw; and when it was bruised they broke it, or threw it away as useless. But the bruised reed shall not be broken by this divine Shepherd of souls. The music of broken sighs and groans, is indeed all that the broken reed can afford Him; the notes are but low, melancholy, and jarring. And yet He will not break the instrument, but He will repair and tune it, until it is fit to join in the concert of angels on high; and even now its humble strains are pleasing to His ears. Surely every broken heart among us must revive, while contemplating this tender and moving imagery.

The other emblem is equally significant and affecting. The 'smoking flax' shall He not quench. It seems to be an allusion to the wick of a candle or lamp, the flame of which is put out, but it still smokes, and retains a little fire which may be again blown into a flame, or rekindled by the application of more fire. Many such dying snuffs or smoking wicks are to be found in the candlesticks of the churches, and in the lamps of the sanctuary. The flame of divine love is just expiring, it is sunk into the socket of a corrupt heart, and produces no clear, steady blaze, but only an unpleasant smoke, although it shows that a spark of the sacred fire yet remains. Or it produces a faint quivering flame that dies away, then catches and revives, and seems unwilling to be quenched entirely.

The devil and the world raise many storms of temptation to blow it out; and a corrupt heart, like a fountain, pours out water to quench it. But even this smoking flax, this dying snuff, Jesus will not quench, but He blows it up into a flame, and pours in the oil of His grace to recruit and nourish it. He walks among the golden candlesticks, and trims the lamps of His sanctuary. Where He finds empty vessels without oil, or without a spark of heavenly fire, like those of the foolish virgins, He breaks the vessels, or throws them out of His house. But where He finds the least spark of true grace, where He discovers but the glimpse of sincere love to Him, where He sees the principle of true piety, which, though just expiring, yet renders the heart susceptive of divine love, as a candle just put out is easily rekindled; there He will strengthen the things which remain and are ready to die. He will blow up the smoking flax to a lively flame, and cause it to shine brighter and brighter to the perfect day. Where there is the least principle of true holiness, He will nourish it. He will furnish the expiring lamp with fresh supplies of the oil of grace, and of heavenly fire; and all the storms that beat upon it shall not be able to put it out, because sheltered by His hand.

I hope, my dear brethren, some of you begin already to feel the pleasing energy of this text. Are you not ready to say, "Blessed Jesus! is this your true character? Then you are just such a Savior as I need, and I most willingly give up myself to you!" You are sensible you are at best, but a bruised reed, a feeble, shattered, useless thing: an untunable, broken pipe of straw, that can make no proper music for the entertainment of your divine Shepherd. Your heart is at best but smoking flax, where the love of God often appears like an expiring flame that quivers and catches, and hovers over the lamp, just ready to go out. Such some of you probably feel yourselves to be. Well, and what do you think of Christ? "He will not break the bruised reed, nor quench the smoking flax;" and therefore, may not even your guilty eyes look to this gentle Savior with encouraging hope? May you not say to him, with the sweet singer of Israel, in his last moment, "He is all my salvation, and all my desire!" (2 Sam. 23:5).

In prosecuting this subject, I intend to illustrate **the character of a weak believer,** as represented in my text; and then to illustrate the **care and compassion of Jesus Christ** even for such a poor weakling.

I: I AM TO ILLUSTRATE THE CHARACTER OF A WEAK BELIEVER *(as represented in my text, by "a bruised reed, and smoking flax.")*

The metaphor of a **BRUISED REED**, as I observed, seems most naturally to convey the idea of a state of weakness and oppression. And, therefore, in illustrating it, I am naturally led to describe the various weaknesses which a believer sometimes painfully feels, and to point out the heavy burdens which he sometimes groans under; I say sometimes, for at other times even the weak believer finds himself strong, strong in the Lord, and in the power of his might, and strengthened with might by the Spirit in the inner man. The joy of the Lord is his strength: and he "can do all things through Christ who gives me strength." Even the oppressed believer at times feels himself delivered from his burden, and he can lift up his drooping head, and walk upright. But, alas! the burden returns, and crushes him again. And under some burden or other many honest-hearted believers groan out the most part of their lives.

Let us now see what are those weaknesses which a believer feels and laments:

♦ He finds himself weak in *knowledge*; a simple child in the knowledge of God and divine things.

♦ He is weak in *love*; the sacred flame does not rise with a perpetual fervor, and diffuse itself through all his devotions, but at times it languishes and dies away into a smoking snuff.

♦ He is weak in *faith*; he cannot keep a strong hold of the Almighty, cannot suspend his all upon his promises with cheerful confidence, nor build a firm, immovable fabric of hope upon the rock Jesus Christ.

♦ He is weak in *hope*; his hope is dashed with rising billows of fears and jealousies, and sometimes just overwhelmed.

♦ He is weak in *joy*; he cannot extract the sweets of Christianity, nor taste the comforts of his religion.

♦ He is weak in *zeal* for God and the interests of his kingdom; he would wish himself always a flaming seraph, always glowing with zeal, always unwearied in serving his God, and promoting the designs of redeeming love in the world. But, alas! At times his zeal, with his love, languishes and dies away into a smoking snuff.

♦ He is weak in *repentance*; troubled with that plague of plagues, a hard heart.

♦ He is weak in the *conflict with indwelling sin,* that is perpetually making insurrections within him.

♦ He is weak in *resisting temptations*; which crowd upon him from without, and are often likely to overwhelm him.

- ♦ He is weak in *courage* to encounter the king of terrors, and venture through the valley of the shadow of death.

- ♦ He is weak in *prayer,* in importunity, in filial boldness, in approaching the mercy-seat.

- ♦ He is weak in *abilities* to endeavor the conversion of sinners and save souls from death.

In short, he is weak in everything, in which he should be strong. He has indeed, like the church of Philadelphia, a little strength, (Rev. 3:8), and at times he feels it. But oh! it seems to him much too little for the work he has to do.

These weaknesses or defects the believer feels, painfully and tenderly feels, and bitterly laments. A sense of them keeps him upon his guard against temptations: he is not venturesome in rushing into the combat. He would not parley with temptation, but would keep out of its way; nor would he run the risk of a defeat by an ostentatious experiment of his strength. This sense of weakness also keeps him dependent upon divine strength. He clings to that support given to Paul in an hour of hard conflict, "My grace is sufficient for you; for my strength is made perfect in weakness;" and when a sense of his weakness has this happy effect upon him, then with Paul he has reason to say, "When I am weak, then I am strong." (2 Corinthians 12:9, 10).

I say the believer feels and laments these weaknesses; and this is the grand distinction in this case between him and the rest of the world. They are the weak too, much weaker than he; nay, they have, properly, no spiritual strength at all; but, alas! they do not feel their weakness, but the poor vain creatures boast of their strength, and think they can do great things when they are disposed for them. Or if their repeated falls and defeats by temptation extort them to a confession of their weakness, they plead it rather as an excuse, than lament it as at once a crime and a calamity. But the poor believer tries no such artifice to extenuate his guilt. He is sensible that even his weakness itself has guilt in it, and therefore he laments his weakness with sincere sorrow, among his other sins.

Now, have I not delineated the very character of some of you; such weaklings, such frail reeds you feel yourselves to be? Well, hear this kind assurance, "Jesus will not break such a feeble reed, but He will support and strengthen it!" But you perhaps not only feel you are weak, but you are oppressed with some heavy burden or other. You are not only a reed for weakness but you are a bruised reed, trodden under foot, crushed under a load. Even this is no unusual or discouraging case, for the weak believer often feels himself crushed under some heavy burden. The frail reed is often bruised; bruised under a due sense of guilt. Guilt lies heavy at times upon his conscience, and he cannot throw it off. The frail reed is often bruised with a sense of remaining sin, which he finds still strong within him, and which at times prevails, and treads him under foot.

The frail reed is often bruised under a burden of deficiencies: the lack of tenderness of heart, the lack of ardent love to God and mankind, the lack of heavenly-mindedness and victory over the world; the lack of conduct and resolution to direct his behavior in a passage so intricate and difficult, and the lack of nearer fellowship with the Father and his Spirit. In short, a thousand pressing needs crush and bruise him!

He also feels his share of the calamities of life in common with other men. But these burdens I shall take no farther notice of, because they are not peculiar to him as a believer, nor do they lie heaviest upon his heart. He could easily bear up under the calamities of life if his spiritual deficiencies were supplied, and the burden of guilt and sin were removed. Under these last he groans and sinks. Indeed these burdens lie with all their full weight upon the world around him; but they are dead in trespasses and sins, and feel them not: they do not groan under them, nor labor for deliverance from them. They lie contented under them, with more stupidity than beasts of burden, until they sink under the intolerable load into the depth of misery!

But the poor believer is not so insensible, and his tender heart feels the burden and groans under it. "We who are in this tabernacle," says Paul, "do groan, being burdened." (2 Corinthians 5:4). The believer understands feelingly that pathetic exclamation, "O wretched man that I am! Who shall deliver me from the body of this death!" (Romans 7:24). He cannot be easy until his conscience is appeased by a well-attested pardon through the blood of Christ. Also, the sins he feels working within him are a real burden and uneasiness to him, though they should never break out into action, and publicly dishonor his holy profession. And is not this the very character of some poor oppressed creatures among you? I hope it is. You may look upon your case to be very discouraging, but Jesus looks upon it in a more favorable light; He looks upon you as proper objects of His compassionate care. Bruised as you are, He will bind up and support you!

I am come to this pass now, that signs will do me no good alone; I have trusted too much to habitual grace for assurance of salvation; I tell you Christ is worth all. He writes, let us see what matter of support and encouragement faith may fetch from Christ's death for justification. And surely that which hath long ago satisfied God himself for the sins of many thousand souls now in heaven, may very well serve to satisfy the heart and conscience of any sinner now upon earth, in any doubts in respect of the guilt of any sins that can arise. - *Thomas Goodwin*

When we hear that Christ was made a curse for us, let us believe it with joy and assurance. By faith Christ changes places with us. He gets our sins, we get His holiness. - *Martin Luther*

O God, we praise Thee for keeping us till this day, and for the full assurance that Thou wilt never let us go. - *C.H. Spurgeon*

Assurance encourages us in our combat; it delivers us not from it. We may have peace with God when we have none from the assaults of Satan. - *John Owen*

O God, we praise Thee for keeping us till this day, and for the full assurance that Thou wilt never let us go. - *C.H. Spurgeon*

DAY 22

THE COMPASSION OF CHRIST TO WEAK BELIEVERS

SAMUEL DAVIES

PART 2

But I proceed to take a view of the character of a weak Christian, as represented in the other metaphor in my text, namely, **SMOKING FLAX**. The idea most naturally conveyed by this metaphor is, that of true and sincere grace but languishing and just expiring, like a candle just blown out, which still smokes and retains a feeble spark of fire. It signifies a susceptibility of enlarged grace, or a readiness to catch that sacred fire, as a candle just put out is easily re-kindled. This metaphor therefore leads me to describe the reality of religion in a low degree, or to delineate the true Christian in his most languishing hours. And in so doing I shall mention those dispositions and exercises which the weakest Christian feels, even in these melancholy seasons; for even in these he widely differs still from the most polished hypocrite in his highest improvements.

ON THIS SUBJECT let me solicit your most serious attention; for, if you have the least spark of real religion within you, you are now likely to discover it, as I am not going to rise to the high attainments of Christians of the first rank, but to stoop to the character of the lowest. Now the peculiar dispositions and exercises of heart which such in some measure feel, you may discover from the following short history of their case:

The weak Christian in such languishing hours does indeed sometimes fall into such a state of carelessness and insensibility, that he has very few and but superficial exercises of mind about divine things. But generally he feels an uneasiness, an emptiness, an anxiety within, under which he droops and pines away, and all the world cannot heal the disease! He has chosen the blessed God as his supreme happiness; and, when he cannot derive happiness from that source, all the sweets of created enjoyments become insipid to him, and cannot fill up the great void which the absence of the Supreme Good leaves in his craving soul. Sometimes his anxiety is indistinct and confused, and he hardly knows what ails him; but at other times he feels it is for God, the living God, that his soul pants. The evaporations of this smoking flax naturally ascend towards heaven. He knows that he never can be happy until he can enjoy the communications of divine love. Let him turn which way he will; he can find no solid ease, no rest, until he comes to this center again.

Even at such times, he cannot be thoroughly reconciled to his sins. He may be parleying with some of them in an unguarded hour, and seem to be negotiating a peace; but the truce is soon ended, and they are at variance again. The enmity of a renewed heart soon rises against this old enemy. And there is this circumstance remarkable in the believer's hatred and opposition to sin, that they do not proceed principally, much less entirely, from a fear of punishment, but from a generous sense to its intrinsic vileness and ingratitude, and its contrariety to the holy nature of God. This is the ground of his hatred to sin, and sorrow for it; and this shows that there is at least a spark of true grace in his heart, and that he does not act altogether from the base, selfish and mercenary principles of mere human nature.

At such times he is very jealous of the sincerity of his religion, afraid that all his past experiences were delusive, and afraid that, if he should die in his present state, he would be forever miserable. A very anxious state is this!

The insensible world can lie secure, while this grand concern lies in the most dreadful suspense. But the tenderhearted believer is not capable of such fool-hardiness: he shudders at the thought of everlasting separation from that God and Savior whom he loves. He loves him, and therefore the fear of separation from him, fills him with all the anxiety of bereaved love. This to him, is the most painful ingredient of the punishment of hell. Hell would be a sevenfold hell to a lover of God, because it is a state of banishment from him whom he loves! He could forever languish and pine away under the consuming distresses of widowed love, which those who love him cannot feel. And has God kindled the sacred flame in his heart, only in order to render him capable of the more exquisite pain? Will he exclude from his presence, the poor creature that clings to him, and languishes for him? No! the flax that does but smoke with his love, was never intended to be fuel for hell; but God will blow it up into a flame, and nourish it until it mingles with the seraphic ardors in the region of perfect love!

The weak believer seems sometimes driven by the tempest of lusts and temptation from off the rock of Jesus Christ. But he makes towards it on the stormy billows, and labors to lay hold upon it, and recover his station there; for he is sensible there is no other foundation of safety; but that without Christ he must perish forever.

It is the habitual disposition of the believer's soul; to depend upon Jesus Christ alone. He retains a kind of inclination or tendency towards him, like the compass needle turns towards the north pole; and, if his heart is turned from its course, it trembles and quivers until it gains its favorite point again, and fixes there. Sometimes, indeed, a consciousness of guilt renders him shy of his God and Savior; and after such base ingratitude he is ashamed to go to him: but at length necessity as well as inclination constrains him, and he is obliged to cry out, "Lord, to whom shall I go? You have the words of eternal life!" (John 6:68). "In you alone I find rest to my soul; and therefore to you I must fly, though I am ashamed and confounded to appear in your presence!"

In short, the weakest Christian upon earth sensibly feels that his comfort rises and falls, as he lives nearer to or farther from his God. The love of God has such a habitual predominance even in his heart, that nothing in the world, nor even all the world together, can fill up God's place. No, when God is gone, heaven and earth together cannot replenish the mighty void.

The weakest Christian upon earth, longs to be delivered from sin, from all sin, without exception: and the body of death hanging about him is the burden of his life.

The poor languishing Christian has his hope, all the little hope that he has, built upon Jesus Christ. This smoking flax sends up some exhalations of love towards heaven. The poor creature that often fears he is altogether a slave to sin; honestly, though feebly, labors to be holy, to be holy as an angel, yes, to be holy as God is holy. He has a heart that feels the attractive charms of holiness, and he is so captivated by it, that sin can never recover its former place of dominion in his heart. No! the tyrant is forever dethroned, and the believer would rather die than yield himself a devoted slave to sin's usurped tyranny again. Thus I have delineated to you, in the plainest manner I could, the character of a weak Christian. Some of you, I am afraid, cannot lay claim even to this low character. If so, you may be sure you are not true Christians, even of the lowest rank. You may be sure you have not the least spark of true religion in your hearts, but are utterly destitute of it.

But some of you, I hope, can say, "Well, after all my doubts and fears, if this is the character of a true, though weak Christian, then I may humbly hope that I am one. I am indeed confirmed in it, that I am less than the least of all other saints upon the face of the earth, but yet I see that I am a saint; for thus has my heart been exercised, even in my dark and languishing hours. This secret uneasiness and pining anxiety, this thirst for God; for the living God, this tendency of soul towards Jesus Christ, this implacable enmity to sin, this panting and struggling after holiness: these things have I often felt!"

And have you indeed? Then away with your doubts and jealousies; away with your fears and despondencies! There is at least an immortal spark kindled in your hearts, which the united power of men and devils, of sin and temptation, shall never be able to quench! No, it shall yet rise into a flame, and burn with seraphic ardors forever! For your farther encouragement, I proceed;

II. TO ILLUSTRATE THE CARE AND COMPASSION OF JESUS CHRIST FOR SUCH POOR WEAKLINGS AS YOU

This may appear a needless task to some: for who is there that does not believe it? But to such would I say, it is no easy thing to establish a trembling soul in the full belief of this truth. It is easy for one that does not see his danger, and does not feel his extreme need of salvation, and the difficulty of the work, to believe that Christ is willing and able to save him. But oh! to a poor soul, deeply sensible of its condition, this is no easy matter. Besides, the heart may need be more deeply affected with this truth, though the understanding should need no farther arguments of the speculative kind for its conviction; and to impress this truth is my present design. For this purpose I need but read and paraphrase to you a few of the many kind declarations and assurances which Jesus has given us in his word, and relate the happy experiences of some of his saints there recorded, who found him true and faithful to his word.

The Lord Jesus Christ seems to have a peculiar tenderness for the poor, the mourners, the broken-hearted; and these are peculiarly the objects of his mediatorial office. "The Spirit of the Sovereign LORD is upon me, because the LORD has appointed me to bring good news to the poor. He has sent me to comfort the brokenhearted and to announce that captives will be released and prisoners will be freed. He has sent me to tell those who mourn that the time of the LORD's favor has come, and with it, the day of God's anger against their enemies. To all who mourn in Israel, he will give beauty for ashes, joy instead of mourning, praise instead of despair. For the LORD has planted them like strong and graceful oaks for his own glory." (Isaiah 61:1-3).

Thus says the LORD, in strains of majesty that become him, "Heaven is my throne, and the earth is my footstool. Could you ever build me a temple as good as that? Could you build a dwelling place for me? My hands have made both heaven and earth, and they are mine. I, the LORD, have spoken!" Had he spoken uniformly in this majestic language to us guilty worms, the declaration might have overwhelmed us with awe but could not have inspired us with hope. But he advances himself thus high; on purpose to let us see how low he can stoop. Hear the encouraging sequel of this his majestic speech: "I will bless those who have humble and contrite hearts, who tremble at my word!" (Isaiah 66:1-2).

He loves to dwell upon this subject, and therefore you hear it again in the same prophecy: "Thus says the high and lofty One who inhabits eternity, whose name is holy," what does he say? "I dwell in the high and holy place." (Isaiah 57:15). This is said of his character; this is a dwelling in some measure worthy the inhabitant. But oh! will he stoop to dwell in a lower mansion, or pitch his tent among mortals? Yes, he dwells not only in his high and holy place but also, "with those whose spirits are contrite and humble. I refresh the humble and give new courage to those with repentant hearts!"

He charges Peter to feed his lambs as well as his sheep; that is, to take the tenderest care even of the weakest in his flock. (John 21:15). And he severely rebukes the shepherds of Israel, "Because," says he, "You have not taken care of the weak. You have not tended the sick or bound up the broken bones. You have not gone looking for those who have wandered away and are lost. Instead, you have ruled them with force and cruelty." (Ezekiel 34:4).

But what an amiable reverse is the character of the great Shepherd and Sustainer of souls! "Behold," says Isaiah, "The Sovereign LORD is coming in all his glorious power. He will rule with awesome strength. See, he brings his reward with him as he comes!" How justly may we tremble at this proclamation of the approaching God! for who can stand when he appears? But how agreeably are our fears quenched in what follows! If he comes to take vengeance on his enemies; he also comes to show mercy to the lowest of his people. "He will feed his flock like a shepherd. He will carry the lambs in his arms, holding them close to his heart. He will gently lead the mother sheep with their young!" (Isaiah 40:10, 11). That is, he shall exercise the tenderest and most compassionate care towards the lowest and weakest of his flock.

"The LORD looked down," says the Psalmist, "from his heavenly sanctuary. He looked to the earth from heaven;" not to view the grandeur and pride of courts and kings, nor the heroic exploits of conquerors, but "to hear the groans of the prisoners, to release those condemned to die!" He will regard the prayer of the destitute, and not despise their prayer. This was written for the generation to come. (Psalm 102:19-20). It was written for your encouragement, my brethren. Over three thousand years ago, this encouraging passage was entered into the sacred records for the support of poor desponding souls today, to the ends of the earth.

Oh, what an early provident care does God show for his people! There are none of the seven churches of Asia so highly commended by Christ as that of Philadelphia; and yet in commending her, all he can say is, "I know all the things you do, and I have opened a door for you that no one can shut. You have little strength, yet you obeyed my word and did not deny me!" (Rev. 3:8).

Oh, how acceptable is a little strength to Jesus Christ, and how ready is he to improve it! "He gives power to those who are tired and worn out", says Isaiah, "He gives strength to the weary and strengthens the powerless!" (Isaiah 40:29). Hear farther what words of grace and truth flowed from the lips of Jesus.

Come to me, all of you who are weary and carry heavy burdens, and I will give you rest. Take my yoke upon you. Let me teach you, because I am humble and gentle, and you will find rest for your souls! - Matthew 11:28-29

All that the Father gives me will come to me, and whoever comes to me I will never drive away! - John 6:37

If anyone is thirsty, let him come to me and drink! - John 7:37

The Spirit and the bride say, "Come!" And let him who hears say, "Come!" Whoever is thirsty, let him come; and whoever wishes, let him take the free gift of the water of life! - Revelation 22:17

Oh, what strong consolation is here! What exceeding great and precious promises are these! I might easily add to the catalogue, but these may suffice. Let us now see how his people in every age have ever found these promises made good.

Here David may be consulted, and he will tell you, pointing to himself, "This poor man cried, and the LORD heard him, and saved him out of all his troubles!" (Psalm 34:6). Paul, in the midst of affliction, calls God "the Father of compassion and the God of all comfort, who comforts us in all our troubles!" (2 Corinthians 1:3, 4). "God," says he, "who comforts those that are cast down has comforted us." (2 Corinthians 7:6). What a sweetly emphatic declaration is this! "God, the comforter of the humble has comforted us!" (This is the literal translation of the text.) He is not only the Lord Almighty, the King of kings, the Creator of the world, but among his more magnificent characters he assumes this title, the Comforter of "the humble."

Such Paul found him in an hour of temptation, when he had this supporting answer to his repeated prayer for deliverance, "My grace is sufficient for you for my power is made perfect in weakness!" (2 Corinthians 12:9). Since this was the case, since his weakness was more than supplied by the strength of Christ, and was a foil to set it off, Paul seems quite regardless what infirmities he labored under. "Therefore I will boast all the more gladly about my weaknesses, so that Christ's power may rest on me. That is why, for Christ's sake, I delight in weaknesses, in insults, in hardships, in persecutions, in difficulties. For when I am weak, then I am strong!" He could take no pleasure in feeling himself weak: but the mortification was made up by the pleasure he found in leaning upon this almighty support. His wounds were painful to him: but, oh! the pleasure he found in feeling the divine physician dressing his wounds, in some measure swallowed up the pain!

It was probably his experience, as well as inspiration, that dictated to the apostle that amiable character of Christ, that he is "A merciful and faithful high priest. Because he himself suffered when he was tempted, he is able to help those who are being tempted." (Hebrews 2:17, 18).

And, "For we do not have a high priest who is unable to sympathize with our weaknesses, but we have one who has been tempted in every way, just as we are yet was without sin." (Hebrews 4:15).

But why need I multiply arguments? Go to his cross and there learn his love and compassion, from his groans and wounds, and blood, and death! Would he hang there in such agony for sinners if he were not willing to save them, and nourish every good principle in them? There you may have much the same evidence of his compassion, as Thomas had of his resurrection: you may look into his hands, and see the print of the nails; and into his side, and see the scar of the spear; which loudly proclaims his readiness to pity and help you!

And now, poor, trembling, doubting souls; you should raise up your drooping head, and take courage! May you not venture your souls into such compassionate and faithful hands? Why should the bruised reed shrink from him, when he comes not to tread it down but raise it up!

As I am really solicitous that impenitent hearts among us should be pierced with the medicinal anguish, and sorrow of conviction, and repentance. I am truly solicitous that every honest soul, in which there is the least spark of true piety, should enjoy the pleasure of it. It is indeed to be lamented that those who have a title to so much happiness, should enjoy so little of it! It is very incongruous that they should go bowing their head in their way towards heaven as if they were hastening to the place of execution! and that they should serve so good a Master, with such heavy hearts! Oh lift up the hands that hang down, and strengthen the feeble knees! "Comfort, comfort my people! says your God." "Be strong in the Lord, and in the power of his might." Trust in your all-sufficient Redeemer; trust in him, though he should slay you!

And do not indulge causeless doubts and fears concerning your sincerity. When they arise in your minds, examine them, and search whether there is any sufficient reason for them; and if you discover there is not, then reject them and set them at defiance, and entertain your hopes in spite of them, and say with the Psalmist, " Why are you downcast, O my soul? Why so disturbed within me? Put your hope in God, for I will yet praise him, my Savior and my God!" (Psalm 42:11).

Faith saves us, but assurance satisfies us. - *C.H. Spurgeon*

True assurance is built upon a Scripture basis: presumption hath no Scripture to show for its warrant; it is like a will without seal and witnesses, which is null and void in law. Presumption wants both the witness of the Word and the seal of the Spirit. Assurance always keeps the heart in a lowly posture; but presumption is bred of pride. Feathers fly up, but gold descends; he who hath this golden assurance, his heart descends in humility. - *Thomas Watson*

To be assured of our salvation is no arrogant stoutness; it is our faith. It is no pride; it is devotion. It is no presumption; it is God's promise.
- *Augustine*

If the ground of our assurance rested in and on ourselves, it might justly be called presumption; but the Lord and the power of His might being the ground thereof, they either know not what is the might of His power, or else too lightly esteem it, who account assured confidence thereon presumption. - *William Gouge*

A well-grounded assurance is always attended by three fair handmaids: love, humility and holy joy. - *Thomas Brooks*

DAY 23

SHOWING THE DIFFERENCE BETWEEN A TRUE AND A COUNTERFEIT ASSURANCE, BETWEEN SOUND ASSURANCE AND PRESUMPTION

BY THOMAS BROOKS

PART 1

He that spared not his own Son, but delivered him up for us all, how shall he not with him also freely give us all things? Who shall lay anything to the charge of God's elect? [It is] God that justifieth. Who [is] he that condemneth? [It is] Christ that died, yea rather, that is risen again, who is even at the right hand of God, who also maketh intercession for us. - Romans 8:32-34

THE FIRST DIFFERENCE: *A sound and well-grounded assurance is attended with a deep admiration of God's transcendent love and favour to the soul in the Lord Jesus.* The assured soul is often a-breathing it out thus: Ah, Lord! who am I, what am I, that thou shouldst give into my bosom, the white stone of absolution, when the world hath given into their bosoms only the black stone of condemnation? Rev. ii. 17. Lord! what mercy is this, that thou shouldst give me assurance, give me water out of the rock, and feed me with manna from heaven, when many of thy dearest ones spend their days in sighing, mourning and complaining for want of assurance. Lord! what manner of love is this, that thou shouldst set me upon thy knee, embrace me in thy arms, lodge me in thy bosom, and kiss me with the sweet kisses of thy blessed mouth, with those kisses that are 'better than wine,' Cant. i 2, yea, better than life, when many are even weary of their lives because they want what I enjoy? Ps. lxiii. 3. Ah, Lord! by what name shall I call this mercy, this assurance that thou hast given me? It being a mercy that fits me to do duties, to bear crosses and to improve mercies; that fits me to speak sweetly, to judge righteously, to give liberally, to act seriously, to suffer cheerfully, and to walk humbly. I cannot, says the assured soul, but sing it out with Moses, 'Who is like unto thee; O Lord, amongst the gods? Who is like thee, glorious in holiness, fearful in praises, doing wonders?' Exod. xv. 2. And with the apostle, 'Oh, the height, the depths, the length and breadth of the love of Christ, which passeth knowledge,' Eph. iii. 18, 19. If the queen of Sheba, says the assured soul, was so swallowed up in a deep admiration of Solomon's wisdom, greatness, goodness, excellency and glory, that she could not but admiringly breathe it thus out, 'Happy are thy men, happy are these thy servants, which stand continually before thee, and that hear thy wisdom,' 1 Kings x. 8, Oh then, how should that blessed assurance that I have of the love of God, of my interest in God, of my union and communion with God, of my blessedness here and my happiness hereafter, work me to a deep and serious, to a real and perpetual, admiration of God.

THE SECOND DIFFERENCE: *Secondly, a well-grounded assurance doth always beget in the soul an earnest and an impatient longing after a further, a clearer, and fuller enjoyment of God and Christ.* Ps. lxiii. 1, 'O God, thou art my God' here is assurance; well, what follows? 'early will I seek thee. My soul thirsteth for thee; my flesh longeth for thee in a dry and thirsty land, where no water is.' The assured soul cries out, 'I desire to be dissolved, and to be with Christ,' Philip. i. 23; and, 'Make haste, my beloved,' Cant. viii. 14; and, 'Come, Lord Jesus, come quickly,' Rev. xxii. 17. O Lord Jesus, says the assured soul, thou art my light, thou art my life, thou art my love, thou art my joy, thou art my crown, thou art my heaven, thou art my all. I cannot but long to see that beautiful face that was spit upon for my sins, and that glorious head that was crowned with thorns for my transgressions. I long to take some turns with thee in paradise, to see the glory of thy Jerusalem above, to drink of those rivers of pleasures that be at thy right hand, to taste of all the delicates of thy kingdom, and to be acquainted with those secrets and mysteries that have been hid from all ages, and to be swallowed up in the full enjoyment of thy blessed self; Eph. iii. 5, Col. i. 26.

THE THIRD DIFFERENCE: *Thirdly, a well-grounded assurance is usually strongly assaulted by Satan on all sides.* Satan is such a grand enemy to joy and peace, to the salvation and consolation, of the saints, that he cannot but make use of all his devices and stratagems to amaze and amuse, to disturb and disquiet, the peace and rest of their souls. No sooner had Jesus Christ heard that lovely voice from heaven, 'This is my beloved Son, in whom I am well pleased,' Mat. iii. 17 and iv. 1, 2, &c., but he is desperately assaulted by Satan in the wilderness. No sooner was Paul dropped out of heaven, after he had seen such visions of glory that was unutterable, but he was presently assaulted and buffeted by Satan, 2 Cor. ii. 12. Stand up, stand up, assured Christians, and tell me whether you have not found the blast of the terrible one to be as a storm against the wall, Isa. xxv. Since the Lord said unto you, Be of good cheer, your sins are forgiven you, have not you found Satan to play the part both of the lion and the wolf, of the serpent and the fox? And all to weaken your assurance, and to work you to question the truths of your assurance, and to cast water upon your assurance, and to take off the freshness and sweetness, the beauty and glory, of your assurance; I know you have. His malice, envy, and enmity is such against God's honour and glory, and your comfort and felicity, that he cannot but be very studious and industrious to make use of all traps, snares, methods, and ways whereby he may shake the pillars of your faith, and weaken and overthrow your assurance. Pirates, you know, do most fiercely assault those ships and vessels that are most richly laden; so doth Satan those precious souls that have attained to the riches of full assurance.

Assurance makes a paradise in believers' souls, and this makes Satan to roar and rage. Assurance fits a man to do God the greatest service and Satan the greatest disservice, and this makes him mad against the soul. Assurance makes a saint to be too hard for Satan at all weapons, yea, to lead that 'son of the morning' captive, to spoil him of all his hurting power, to bind him in chains, and to triumph over him; and this makes his hell a great deal hotter, Rom. viii. 32-39. And therefore never wonder at Satan's assaulting your assurance, but expect it and look for it. The jailor is quiet when his prisoner is in bolts, but if he be escaped then he pursues him with hue and cry. So long as the soul is in bolts and bondage under Satan, Satan is quiet and is not so apt to molest and vex it; but when once a soul is made free, and assured of his freedom by Christ, John viii. 36, then says Satan, as once Pharaoh did, 'I will arise, I will pursue, I will overtake, I will divide the spoil; my lust shall be satisfied upon them; I will draw my sword, my hand shall destroy them,' Exodus xv. 9. The experience of all assured saints doth abundantly confirm this. Israel going into Egypt had no enemies, no opposition, but travelling into Canaan they were never free.

THE FOURTH DIFFERENCE: *Fourthly, a well-grounded assurance makes a man as bold as a lion; it makes him valiant and gallant for Christ and his cause, in the face of all dangers and deaths.* After the Holy Ghost was fallen upon the apostles, and had assured them of their internal and eternal happiness, oh! how bold, how undaunted, how resolute were they in the face of all oppositions, afflictions, and persecutions! as you may see from the second of the Acts of the Apostles to the end of the Acts. So assurance had this operation upon David's heart: Ps. xxiii. 4, 6 compared, 'Surely goodness and mercy shall follow me all the days of my life.' Well, David, but how doth this assurance of yours operate? Why, saith he 'Though I walk through the valley of the shadow of death, I will fear no evil.' So Moses having an assurance of the 'recompence of reward,' he fears not the wrath of the king, 'for he endured, as seeing him who is invisible,' Heb. xi. 26, 27. So in Heb. x. 34, 'And ye took joyfully the spoiling of your goods, knowing in yourselves that ye have in heaven a better and an enduring substance.' Oh, that knowledge, that assurance that they had in their own hearts of enjoying in heaven a better and a more enduring substance, made them bear cheerfully and gallantly the spoiling of their worldly goods. Though the archers (the world, the flesh, and the devil) do shoot sore at a soul under assurance, yet his bow will still abide in strength. Assurance will make a man to break a bow of steel, to trample down strength, and to triumph over all oppositions and afflictions.

Colonus the Dutch martyr called to the judge that had sentenced him to death, and desired him to lay his hand upon his heart, and asked him whose heart did most beat, his or the judge's. Assurance will make a man do this, and much more for Christ and his cause.

THE FIFTH DIFFERENCE: *Fifthly, a well-grounded assurance of a man's own eternal happiness and blessedness will make him very studious and laborious to make others happy.* Ps. lxvi. 16, 'Come and hear, all ye that fear God, and I will tell you what he hath done for my soul.' I will acquaint you with the soul blessings, with the soul favours, that God hath crowned me with. I was darkness, but he hath made me light; I was unrighteousness, but he hath made me righteous; I was deformed, but he hath made me complete; I was full of sores, and spots, and blemishes, but he hath washed me, and made me all fair, without spot or wrinkle. I have found the want of assurance, I now see the worth of assurance; I have long sought assurance, and now I find the sweetness of assurance. Ah! it is such a pearl of price, it is such a beam of God, it is such a spark of glory, that makes my soul a rich amends for all its waiting, weeping, and wrestling.

So, when it pleased God to call Paul by his grace, and to reveal Christ in him and to him, ah! how doth he labour, as for life, to bring others to an acquaintance with Christ, and to an acceptance of Christ, and to an assurance of everlasting happiness and blessedness by Christ! After Paul had been in paradise, he makes it his all to bring others to paradise, 2 Cor. xii. So the spouse in the Canticles, having assurance of her interest in Christ, how doth she labour, by all holy and heavenly rhetoric and logic, by all the strains of love and sweetness, to draw the daughters of Jerusalem to a sight of Christ, Cant. v. 10-16, and vi. 1, &c. When a beam of divine light and love had shined upon Andrew, he labours to draw his brother Simon to the fountain of all light and love, John i. 40-42. And when Philip had but a cast of Christ's countenance, his pulse beats, and his heart calls upon Nathanael to come and share with him in that lovingkindness that was better than life, John i. 43-47.

The constant cry of souls under the power of assurance is, 'Come, taste and see how good the Lord is,' Ps. xxxiv. 8. Ah, sinners, sinners! 'His ways are ways of pleasantness, and all his paths are peace,' Prov. iii. 17; His 'commands are not grievous,' 1 John v. 3, but joyous; 'his yoke is easy, and his burden is light,' Mat. xi. 30; not only for keeping, but also 'in keeping of his commands there is great reward,' Ps. xix. 11. Assurance will strongly put men upon winning of others by counsel, by example, by prayer, and by communicating their spiritual experiences to them. Assurance will furnish a man with will, skill, and experience to confute all those false reports that vain men frequently cast upon the Lord and his ways. It will make a man proclaim to the world 'that one day in the Lord's courts is better than a. thousand years elsewhere,' Ps. lxxxiv. 10; that there are more glorious joys, more pure comforts, more abiding peace, more royal contents, more celestial delights, in one day's walking with God, in one hour's communion with God, &c., than is to be found in all things below God. And by these and such like ways, souls under the power of a well-grounded assurance do endeavour to make others happy with themselves. A soul under assurance is unwilling to go to heaven without company. He is often a-crying out, Father, bless this soul too, and crown that soul too let us to heaven together, let us be made happy together.

THE SIXTH DIFFERENCE: *Sixthly, a well-grounded assurance of God's love, and of a man's everlasting happiness and blessedness, will exceedingly arm and strengthen him against all wickedness and baseness (Ezek. xvi. 60-63.)* No man loathes sin, and himself for sin, as such a man; no man wars and watches against sin more than such a man; no man sighs and mourns, bleeds and complains, under the sense of sinful motions and sinful operations more than such a man, Luke vii. 44, 50. Every stirring of sin makes a man that is under the power of assurance to cry out, 'O wretched man that I am, who shall deliver me from this body of death?' Rom. vii. 22-25: Ps. lxxxv. 8, 'I will hear what God the Lord will speak; for he will speak peace unto his people, and to his saints: and let them not turn again to folly,' or, as the Hebrew will bear, 'And they shall not return to folly.' God's speaking peace to his people fences and fortifies them against folly and vanity.

The assurance that Joseph had of his master's love armed him against the lascivious assaults of his lustful mistress; and will not divine love, that is stronger than death, do this and more? Cant. viii. 6, 7. Assurance makes a man say to his sins, as be to his idols, 'Get you hence, for what have I any more to do with idols?' So says the assured soul, Away pride, away passion, away worldly-mindedness, away uncleanness, away uncharitableness, &c., for what have I any more to do with you? Assurance makes the soul speak to sin as David speaks to sinners: Ps. cxix. 115, 'Depart from me, ye workers of iniquity; for I will keep the commandments of my God:' so says the assured soul, Depart from me, O my lusts, for I have tasted of the love of God, and I have given up myself wholly and only to God, and I cannot but keep the commandments of my God. The Jewish Rabbis report, that the same night that Israel departed out of Egypt towards Canaan, all the idols and idolatrous temples in Egypt, by lightning and earthquakes, were broken down. So when Christ and assurance comes to be set up in the soul, all, the idols of Satan and a man's own heart are cast down, and cast out as an abomination. Sound assurance puts a man upon purifying himself, even as Christ is pure, 1 John iii. 2, 3. The assured Christian knows, that it is dangerous to sin against light, that it is more dangerous to sin against love, that it is most dangerous to sin against love revealed and manifested. God may well say to such a Christian, Is this thy kindness to thy friend? To sin under assurance, is to sin against the bowels of mercy, it is to sin against the highest hopes of glory; and this will certainly provoke God to be angry. 1 Kings xi. 9, 'And the Lord was angry with Solomon, because his heart was turned from the Lord God of Israel, that had appeared to him twice.' To sin under assurance, is to sin in paradise; it is to sin under the flaming sword, it is to sin in the suburbs of heaven, it is to run the hazard of losing that favour 'that is better than life,' of that 'joy that is unspeakable and full of glory,' and of that 'peace that passes understanding.' To sin under assurance, is to cast reproach upon Christ, to grieve the Spirit, to wound conscience, to weaken your graces, to blur your evidences, to usher in calamities, to embitter your mercies, and to provoke the tempter to triumph over your Saviour. Verily, that assurance is but presumption that works men to play with sin, to be bold with sin, to make light of sin, to walk on in ways of sin. Such assurance will never bring a man to heaven, it will never keep him from dropping, into hell, yea, it will double his damnation, and make him the most miserable among all damned, miserable, forlorn spirits. Ah, Lord! from such an assurance deliver my soul; and give me more and more of that divine assurance that makes sin to be more hateful than hell, and that makes the soul to be more careful to avoid the one, than it is fearful of falling into the other.

Reason's arm is too short to reach the jewel of assurance. - *Thomas Brooks*

The cross which is the object of faith, is also, by the power of the Holy Spirit, the cause of it. Sit down and watch the dying Savior till faith springs up spontaneously in your heart. There is no place like Calvary for creating confidence. The air of that sacred hill brings health to trembling faith. Many a watcher there has said: "While I view Thee, wounded, grieving, Breathless on the cursed tree, Lord, I feel my heart believing That Thou suffer'dst thus for me." - *C.H. Spurgeon*

A well-grounded assurance of heaven and happiness, instead of puffing a man up with pride, will make and keep him very humble. - *Matthew Henry*

Faith is our seal; assurance of faith is God's seal. - *Christopher Nesse*

Assurance grows by repeated conflict, by our repeated experimental proof of the Lord's power and goodness to save; when we have been brought very low and helped, sorely wounded and healed, cast down and raised again, have given up all hope, and been suddenly snatched from danger, and placed in safety; and when these things have been repeated to us and in us a thousand times over, we begin to learn to trust simply to the word and power of God, beyond and against appearances: and this trust, when habitual and strong, bears the name of assurance; for even assurance has degrees. - *John Newton*

DAY 24

SHOWING THE DIFFERENCE BETWEEN A TRUE AND A COUNTERFEIT ASSURANCE, BETWEEN SOUND ASSURANCE AND PRESUMPTION

BY THOMAS BROOKS

PART 2

THE SEVENTH DIFFERENCE: *Seventhly, a well-grounded assurance is always attended with three fair handmaids, or with three sweet companions:*

The first handmaid. The first is **love**. Oh! the assurance of divine favour doth mightily inflame a man's love to Christ. Mary Magdalene loved much; Christ's love to her drew out her, love very much to Christ, Luke vii. Assurance makes the soul sing it out with that sweet singer of Israel, 'I will dearly love thee, O Lord, my strength,' Ps. xviii. 2. Lovers know not how to keep silence; lovers of Christ are full of gracious expressions. *Magnes amoris est amor*, love is the attractive loadstone of love. It is impossible for a soul not to love Christ, that knows he is beloved of Christ. Christ's love constrains the soul to love, not by forcible but loving necessity. Praxiteles, the sculptor, exquisitely drew love, taking the pattern from that passion which he felt in his own heart. A believer cannot find the heart of Christ to be beating towards him, but his heart will strongly beat towards Christ. Divine love is like a rod of myrtle, which, as Pliny reports, makes the traveller that carries it in his hand, that he shall never be faint, weary of walking, or loving. Love alone overpowereth all power. Love is the diadem; none but the queen must wear it. Love is the wedding garment; none but the spouse can fit it. Love is a loadstone to draw, as well as a fire to warm. He that doth not love Christ, was never assured of the love of Christ.

The second handmaid, or companion that attends a well-grounded assurance, is **humility.** David, under assurance, cries out, 'I am a worm and no man,' Ps. xxii. 6; Abraham, under assurance, cries out, that he is but 'dust and ashes;' Jacob, under assurance, cries out, that he was 'less than the least of all mercies;' Job, under assurance, 'abhors himself in dust and ashes;' Moses had the honour and the happiness to speak with God 'face to face;' he was very much in God's books, in God's favour; and yet a more humble soul the earth did never bear. The great apostle Paul, under all the revelations and glorious manifestations of God to him, counts himself 'less than the least of all saints,' Eph. iii. 8. That is presumption, that is a delusion of the devil, and no sound assurance, that puffs and swells the souls of men, that makes men prize themselves above the market, above the value that God hath put upon them.

The third handmaid or companion that attends assurance, is **holy joy**. Ah! this assurance causes the strong waters of consolation to overflow the soul. Assurance raises the strongest joy in the soul: Luke i. 46, 47, and Mary said, 'My soul doth magnify the Lord, and my spirit hath rejoiced in God my Saviour.' When a man comes to be assured that God is his Saviour, presently his spirit rejoices in God. This truth is held forth by three parables in that of Luke xv., so in that of 1 Peter i. 8, 9, 'Whom having not seen, ye love; in whom, though now ye see him not, yet believing, ye rejoice with joy unspeakable, and full of glory: receiving the end of your faith, even the salvation of your souls.' Oh the joy, the joy, the inexpressible joy that attends a well-grounded assurance! Assurance raises a paradise of delight in the soul.

> *In quibus operamur, in illis et gaudemus, saith Tertullian:*
> *In what things or persons we act, in those things we rejoice.*

A Christian, under the power of assurance, works all his works in Christ; in him, therefore, and in him alone, he rejoiceth.

THE EIGHTH DIFFERENCE: *Eighthly, and lastly, a well-grounded assurance sometimes springs from the testimony and witness of the Spirit of God.* The Spirit sometimes witnesses to a believer's spirit that he is born of God, that he is beloved of God, that he hath union and communion with God, and that he shall reign forever with God: Rom. viii. 26, 'The Spirit itself beareth witness with our spirits, that we are the children of God.' The Spirit itself witnesseth not only the gifts and graces of the Spirit, but the Spirit itself witnesseth together with our own spirit, that we are the children of God. Sometimes the saints have two witnesses joining their testimonies together to confirm and establish them in these blessed and glorious truths, that they are the sons of God and heirs of glory; and this is their honour as well as their comfort, that the blessed Spirit should bear witness at the bar of their consciences that they are the sons of God: 1 Cor. ii. 12, 'Now we have received, not the spirit of the world, but the Spirit which is of God; that we might know the things that are freely given to us of God;' that is, that we may know our election, vocation, justification, sanctification, and glorification. A man may receive many things that are freely given of God, and yet not know them till the Spirit comes and makes them known to the soul.

Question: But you may say to me, How shall we know the whispering of the Holy Spirit from the hissing of the old serpent? How shall we know the report, the witness, and testimony of the Spirit of Christ, from that report, witness, and testimony that the old serpent deludes and deceives many by, in these days wherein he mostly appears in his angelical robes?

Answer: I answer, you may know the whispering of the Spirit from the hissing of the old serpent, &c., by these following things, which I desire that you would seriously consider, as you tender the peace and settlement, the satisfaction, consolation, and salvation of your own souls.

The first difference: First, The Spirit of Christ doth not witness by any outward voice, as God did from heaven of Christ, Mat. iii. 17; nor by an angel, as to the Virgin Mary, Luke i. 30-34; but by an inward, secret, glorious, and unspeakable way he bids believers be of good cheer, their sins are forgiven them, as Christ said to the palsied man in the Gospel, Mat. ix. 2. And this truth is to be solemnly minded against those poor deceived and deluded souls in these days, that would make the world believe that they have had such and such glorious things made known by an outward, audible voice from heaven. It is much to be feared that they never found the inward, the sweet, the secret, the powerful testimony and report of the Spirit of Christ, that boast, and brag, and rest so much upon an outward testimony. In 1 Kings xix. 11-13, you read of 'a great strong wind that rent the mountains, and brake in pieces the rocks: but the Lord was not in the wind: and after the wind there was an earthquake; but the Lord was not in the earthquake: and after the earthquake a fire; but the Lord was not in the fire: and after the fire there was a still small voice,' and the Lord spake to Elijah in that still small voice. Ah, Christians! the Spirit of the Lord makes not a noise, but he comes in a still small voice, as I may say, and makes a soft and secret report to the soul, that it is beloved, that it is pardoned, and that it shall be forever glorified.

The second difference: Secondly, The testimony and witness of the Spirit of Christ is only gained and enjoyed in holy and heavenly ways, as you may clearly see by comparing the Scriptures in the margin together. The Spirit of the Lord is a Holy Spirit, and he cannot, he will not make any report of the love of the Father to the soul out of a way of holiness. Verily, all those glorious reports that many boast they have met with in sinful ways, in wretched and ungodly ways, are from the hissing of the old serpent, and not from the whisperings of the Spirit of grace. I think it is little less than blasphemy for any to affirm, that the blessed Spirit of Christ doth make reports of the love and favour of God to persons walking in ways of wickedness and baseness.

The third difference: Thirdly, The testimony and witness of the Spirit of Christ, is a clear, a full, a satisfying testimony and witness, John xiv. 17, 1 John iii. 24. The soul sits down under the home-reports of the Spirit, and saith, Lord, it is enough; the soul being full, sits down and sweetly sings it out: 'My beloved is mine, and I am his. I am my well-beloved's, and his desire is towards me,' Cant. ii. 16, and vii. 10. 'The Lord is my portion and the lot of mine inheritance,' Ps. xvi. 5. 'I have none in heaven but thee, neither is there any on earth that I desire in comparison of thee,' Ps. lxxiii. 25. 'Henceforth is laid up for me a crown of righteousness,' 2 Tim. iv. 8. 'Make haste, my beloved,' &c., Cant. viii.

14. Such power, majesty, and glory, attends the glorious testimony of the Spirit of Christ, as scatters all clouds, as resolves all doubts, as answers all objections, as silences the wrangling soul, &c. If the testimony of the Spirit of Christ were not a full, satisfying testimony, it could never fill the soul with such joy as is 'unspeakable and full of glory,' and with 'such peace as passes understanding;' if the testimony were not satisfactory, the soul would still be under fears and doubts, the heart would still be a-wrangling and quarrelling, I may perish, and I may be undone, I may have the door of mercy shut against me, &c. If you bring news to a condemned person that the king hath pardoned him, and that he will receive him to favour, and confer such and such dignity upon him, yet this doth not quiet him nor satisfy him, till he knows it is the king's act, till he is satisfied in that, he cannot say it is enough, he cannot be cheerful, he cannot be delightful, &c. But when he is satisfied that it is the king's act, that the king hath certainly done this and that for him, then he is satisfied, and then sighing and mourning flies away, and then he rejoices with joy unspeakable. So it is with a believing soul under the testimony and witness of the spirit of Christ.

The fourth difference: Fourthly, Though the Spirit be a witnessing Spirit, yet he doth not always witness to believers their adoption, their interest in Christ, &c. There is a mighty difference between the working of the Spirit and the witness of the Spirit. There are oftentimes many glorious and efficacious works of the Spirit, as faith, love, repentance, holiness, &c., where there is not the witness of the Spirit, Isa. 11:2. David at that very time had the Spirit, and many sweet workings of the Spirit in him and upon him, when he had by sin lost the witness and testimony of the Spirit, Ps. li. 10-12. Though the Spirit of the Lord be a witnessing and a sealing Spirit, yet he doth not always witness and seal up the love and favour of the Father to believers' souls, as you may see by the scriptures in the margin, and as the experience of many precious Christians can abundantly evidence. All believers do not see alike need of this testimony, they do not all alike prize this testimony, they do not all alike observe it and improve it; and therefore, it is no wonder if the Spirit be a witnessing Spirit to some and not to others. You do but gratify Satan and wrong your own souls, when you argue that certainly you have not the Spirit, because he is not a witnessing and a sealing Spirit to your souls. Though it be the office of the Spirit to witness, yet it is not his office always to witness to believers their happiness and blessedness. The Spirit may act one way and in one room of the soul, when he doth not act in another. Sometimes the Spirit works upon the understanding, sometimes upon the will, sometimes upon the affections, sometimes upon faith, sometimes upon fear, sometimes upon love, sometimes upon humility, &c. Our hearts are the Spirit's harps. If a man should always touch one string in an instrument, he should never play various tunes, he should never make pleasant music; no more would the Spirit, if he should be always a-doing one thing in the soul. Therefore he acts variously. Sometimes he will shew himself a quickening Spirit, sometimes an enlightening Spirit, sometimes a rejoicing Spirit, sometimes a sealing Spirit, and always a supporting Spirit, &c.

The fifth difference: Fifthly, The testimony and witness of the Spirit is a sure testimony, a sure witness. The Spirit is truth itself; he is the great searcher of the deep things of God. The Spirit of the Lord is the discoverer, the confuter, and destroyer of all false spirits. The Spirit is above all possibility of being deceived, he is omnipotent, he is omniscient, he is omnipresent, he is one of the cabinet council of heaven; he lies and lives in the bosom of the Father, and can call them all by name upon whom the Father hath set his heart, and therefore his testimony must needs be true. It is a surer testimony than if a man should hear a voice from heaven pronouncing him to be happy and blessed. You may safely and securely lay the weight of your souls upon this testimony; it never hath, it never will deceive any that hath leaned upon it. This testimony will be a rock that will bear up a soul, when other false testimonies will be but 'a reed of Egypt,' that will deceive the soul, that will undo the soul; as I am afraid many in this deluding age have found by sad experience.

The sixth difference: Sixthly, The testimony of God's Spirit is always accompanied with the testimony of our own. These may be distinguished, but they can never be separated. When the Spirit of God gives in witness for a man, his own spirit doth not give in witness against him. Look, as face answers to face, so doth the witness of a believer's spirit answer to the witness of the Spirit of Christ. Rom. viii. 16, 'The Spirit witnesseth together with our spirits that we are the sons of God.' Now, if our own consciences do not testify first, that we are sons and heirs, the Spirit doth not testify; for the Spirit bears witness together with our spirits. St John is very express in 1 John iii. 21, 'But if our hearts condemn us not, then have we confidence toward God. But if our hearts condemn us, God is greater than our hearts, and knoweth all things.' 1 John v. 8-12, and 'There are three that bear witness in earth, the Spirit, and the water, and the blood, and these three agree in one.' The Spirit doth witness eminently and efficiently, but water and blood materially, and our spirits and reason instrumentally. By the Spirit we may understand the Holy Ghost, by whose strength we lay hold on Christ and all his benefits. By water we may understand our regeneration, our sanctification; and by blood we may understand the blood and righteousness of Christ, that is imputed and applied by faith to us. 'And these three agree in one,' that is, they do all three of one accord testify the same thing.

The seventh difference: Seventhly, The witness of the Spirit
is ever according to the word. There is a sweet harmony between the
inward and the outward testimony, between the Spirit of God and the
word of God. The scriptures were all composed by the Spirit, 2 Peter i.
20, 21; and therefore the Spirit cannot contradict himself, which he
should do, if he should give in any testimony contrary to the testimony
of the word. It is blasphemy to make the testimony of the Spirit to
contradict the testimony of the word. The Spirit hath revealed his whole
mind in the word, and he will not give a contrary testimony to what he
hath given in the word. The word saith, They that are born again, that are
new creatures, that believe and repent, shall be saved. But thou art born
again, thou art a new creature, thou believest and repentest; therefore
thou shalt be saved, saith the Spirit The Spirit never looseth where the
word bindeth, the Spirit never justifies where the word condemns, the
Spirit never approves where the word disapproves, the Spirit never
blesses where the word curses. In the Old Testament all revelations were
to be examined by the word, Deut. xiii. 1-4. Isa. viii. 20, 'To the law and
to the testimony: if they speak not according to this word, it is because
there is no light (or no morning) in them.' So in that of John xvi. 13,
'The Spirit shall lead you into all truth: for he shall not speak of himself;
but what he shall hear, that shall he speak.' Here the Holy Ghost is
brought in as some messenger or ambassador who only relates things
faithfully according to that he hath in charge. Such as look and lean upon
the hissing of the old serpent, may have a testimony that they are happy,
against the testimony of the word; but wherever the Spirit of Christ gives
in his testimony, it is still according to the word. Look, as indenture
answers to indenture, or as the counterpain exactly answers to the
principal conveyance; there is article for article, clause for clause,
covenant for covenant, word for word; so doth the testimony of the
Spirit exactly answer to the testimony of the word.

The eighth difference: Eighthly, It is a holy witness, a holy
testimony. It is formally, it is originally holy, it is effectually holy. Nothing
makes the heart more in the love, study, practice, and growth of holiness,
than the glorious testimony of the Holy Spirit; and the more clear and
full the testimony is, the more holy and gracious it will make the soul.
Nothing puts such golden engagements upon the soul to holiness, as the
Spirit sealing a man up to the day of redemption, as the Spirit speaking
and sealing peace, love, and pardon to the soul, Ps. lxxxv. 8; 1 Cor. xv. 31;
2 Cor. v. 14. Nothing makes a man more careful to please Christ, more
fearful to offend Christ, more studious to exalt Christ, and more
circumspect to walk with Christ, than this testimony of the Spirit of
Christ. Verily, that is not the blessed whispering of Christ's Spirit, but the
hissing of the old serpent, that makes men bold with sin, that makes men
dally with sin, that makes man a servant to sin, that breeds a contempt of

ordinances, a neglect of holy duties, a carelessness in walking with God. And from those hissings of the old serpent, O Lord, deliver my soul, and the souls of all thy servants that put their trust in thee.

The ninth difference: Ninthly and lastly, Assurance is a jewel, a pearl of that price, that God only bestows it upon renewed hearts. The Spirit never sets his seal upon any, but upon those that Christ hath first printed his image upon. God gives to none the white stone, Rev. ii. 17, but to those from whom he hath taken the heart of stone; Ezek. xxxvi. 25, 26, 27 compared. Christ never tells a man that his name is written in the book of life, till he hath breathed into him spiritual life, Luke x. 20. Christ never says, Son, be of good cheer, thy sin is pardoned, till he hath first said, Be thou healed, be thou cleansed, Luke v. 18-20. Christ never gives a man a new name, that is better than the names of sons and daughters, till he hath made them new creatures, Isa. lvi. 5; 2 Cor. v. 17. Of slaves Christ first makes us sons, before we cry Abba, Father, Rom. viii. 15. Of enemies, he first makes us friends, before he will make us of his court or counsel, Eph. ii. 13-20. Christ will never hang a pearl in a swine's snout, nor put new wine into old bottles, nor his royal robes upon a leprous back, nor his golden chain about a dead man's neck, nor his glistening crown upon a traitor's head. The Spirit never sets his seal upon any, but upon those that Christ hath first set as a seal upon his heart, Eph. i. 13; Cant. viii. 6. The Spirit only bears witness to such as hate sin as Christ hates it, and that love righteousness as Christ loves it, that hate sin more than hell, and that love truth more than life, Ps. xlv. 7. A soul sealed by the Spirit will pull out right eyes, and cut off right hands, for Christ such souls will part with a Benjamin, and offer up an Isaac, for Christ. And this is to be seriously minded against those deceived and deluded souls, that remain yet in their blood, and that wallow in their sins, and yet boast and brag of the seal and of the witness and testimony of the Spirit.

And thus I have shewed you the difference between the whisperings of the Spirit and the hissing of the old serpent, between a true testimony and a false.

A believer can sail to heaven, though the tide of reason and the wind of temptation are against him. - *Thomas Watson*

It may be you have been more earnest and vehement for assurance, and the effects of it, viz., joy, comfort, and peace, than you have been for grace and holiness, for communion with God, and conformity to God. It may be your requests for assurance have been full of life and spirits, when your requests for grace and holiness, for communion with God, and conformity to God, have been lifeless and spiritless. If so, no wonder that assurance is denied you. Assurance makes most for your comfort, but holiness makes most for God's honour. Man's holiness is now his greatest happiness, and in heaven man's greatest happiness will be his perfect holiness. - *Thomas Brooks*

A common cause of the absence of assurance is, slothfulness about growth in grace. I suspect many true believers hold dangerous and unscriptural views on this point; I do not of course mean intentionally, but they do hold them. Many appear to think that, once converted, they have little more to attend to, and that a state of salvation is a kind of easy chair, in which they may just sit still, lie back, and be happy. They seem to fancy that grace is given them that they may enjoy it, and they forget that it is given, like a talent, to be used, employed, and improved. Such persons lose sight of the many direct injunctions "to increase, to grow, to abound more and more, to add to our faith," and the like; and in this little-doing condition, this sitting-still state of mind, I never marvel that they miss assurance. - *J.C. Ryle*

When I live in a settled and steadfast assurance about the state of my soul, methinks then I am as bold as a lion. I can laugh at all trouble: no affliction daunts me. But when I am eclipsed in my comforts, I am of so fearful a spirit, that I could run into a very mouse-hole. - *Hugh Latimer*

Assurance will assist us in all duties; it will arm us against all temptations; it will answer all objections; it will sustain us in all conditions into which the saddest of times can bring us. "If God be for us, who can be against us?" - *Bishop Reynolds*

DAY 25

ASSURANCE – 2 TIM 4:6-8
BY J.C. RYLE
PART 1

For I am now ready to be offered, and the time of my departure is at hand. I have fought a good fight, I have finished my course, I have kept the faith: Henceforth there is laid up for me a crown of righteousness, which the Lord, the righteous judge, shall give me at that day: and not to me only, but unto all them also that love his appearing.
- 2 Tim. 4:6-8

READER, OBSERVE THAT THE Apostle speaks without any hesitation or distrust. He regards the crown as a sure thing: as his own already. He declares with unfaltering confidence his firm persuasion that the righteous Judge will give it to him. Paul was no stranger to all the circumstances and accompaniments of that solemn day to which he referred. The great white throne, the assembled world, the open books, the revealing of all secrets, the listening angels, the awful sentence, the eternal separation of the lost and saved, all these were things with which he was well acquainted. But none of these things moved him. His strong faith over-leaped them all, and only saw Jesus, his all-prevailing Advocate, and the blood of sprinkling, and sin washed away. "A crown," he says, "is laid up for me." "The Lord Himself shall give it to me." He speaks as if he saw it all with his own eyes.

Such are the main things which these verses contain. Of most of them I cannot pretend to speak, for space would not allow me. I shall only try to set before you one point in the passage, and that is "the assured hope" with which the Apostle looks forward to his own prospects in the day of judgment. I shall do this the more readily, because of the great importance which I feel attaches to the subject of assurance, and the great neglect with which, I humbly conceive, it is often treated in this day. But I shall do it at the same time with fear and trembling. I feel that I am treading on very difficult ground, and that it is easy to speak rashly and unscripturally in this matter. The road between truth and error is here especially a narrow pass, and if I shall be enabled to do good to some without doing harm to others, I shall be very thankful.

I. FIRST, THEN, I WILL TRY TO SHOW YOU THAT AN ASSURED HOPE IS A TRUE AND SCRIPTURAL THING.

Assurance, such as Paul expresses in the verses which head this tract, is not a mere fancy or feeling. It is not the result of high animal spirits, or a sanguine temperament of body. It is a positive gift of the Holy Ghost, bestowed without reference to men's bodily frames or constitutions, and a gift which *every believer* in Christ ought to aim at and seek after. The Word of God appears to me to teach that a believer may arrive at an assured confidence with regard to his own salvation.

I would lay it down fully and broadly, that a true Christian, a converted man, may reach that comfortable degree of faith in Christ, that in general he shall feel entirely confident as to the pardon and safety of his soul, shall seldom be troubled with doubts, seldom be distracted with hesitation, seldom be distressed by anxious questionings, and, in short, though vexed by many an inward conflict with sin, shall look forward to death without trembling, and to judgment without dismay. Such is my account of assurance. I will ask you to mark it well. I say neither less nor more than I have here laid down.

Now, such a statement as this is often disputed and denied. Many cannot see the truth of it at all. The Church of Rome denounces assurance in the most unmeasured terms. The Council of Trent declares roundly, that a "believer's assurance of the pardon of his sins is a vain and ungodly confidence;" and Cardinal Bellarmine, the well-known champion of Romanism, calls it "a prime error of heretics." The vast majority of the worldly among ourselves oppose the doctrine of assurance. It offends and annoys them to hear of it. They do not like others to feel comfortable and sure, because they never feel so themselves. That they cannot receive it is certainly no marvel.

But there are also some true believers who reject assurance, or shrink from it as a doctrine fraught with danger. They consider it borders on presumption. They seem to think it a proper humility never to be confident, and to live in a certain degree of doubt. This is to be regretted, and does much harm.

I frankly allow there are some presumptuous persons who profess to feel a confidence for which they have no Scriptural warrant. There always are some people who think well of themselves when God thinks ill, just as there are some who think ill of themselves when God thinks well. There always will be such. There never yet was a Scriptural truth without abuses and counterfeits. God's election, man's impotence, salvation by grace, all are alike abused. There will be fanatics and enthusiasts as long as the world stands. But, for all this, assurance is a real, sober, and true thing; and God's children must not let themselves be driven from the use of a truth, merely because it is abused.

My answer to all who deny the existence of real, well-grounded assurance is simply this; What saith the Scripture? If assurance be not there, I have not another word to say.

♦ But does not Job say, "I **know** that my Redeemer liveth, and that He shall stand at the latter day upon the earth: and though after my skin worms destroy this body, yet in my flesh shall I see God"? (Job 19:25-26)

♦ Does not David say, "Though I walk through the valley of the shadow of death, I will *fear no* evil: for Thou art with me; thy rod and Thy staff they comfort me"? (Psalm 23:4)

♦ Does not Isaiah say, "Thou wilt keep him in ***perfect peace*** whose mind is stayed on Thee, because he trusteth in Thee"? (Isaiah 26:3)

♦ And again, "The work of righteousness shall be peace, and the effect of righteousness quietness and *assurance* forever." (Isaiah 32:17)

♦ Does not Paul say to the Romans, "I am ***persuaded*** that neither life, nor death, nor angels, nor principalities, nor powers, nor things present, nor things to come, not height, nor depth, nor any other creature, shall be able to separate us from the love of God, which is in Christ Jesus our Lord"? (Rom. 8:38-39)

♦ Does he not say to the Corinthians, "We *know* that if our earthly house of this tabernacle were dissolved, we have a building of God, a house not made with hands, eternal in the heavens"? (2 Cor. 5:1)

♦ And again, "We are always *confident,* knowing that whilst we are at home in the body, we are absent from the Lord." (2 Cor. 5:6)

♦ Does he not say to Timothy, "I *know* whom I have believed, and am *persuaded* that He is able to keep that which I have committed to Him"? (2 Tim. 1:12)

♦ And does he not speak to the Colossians of "the full *assurance* of understanding" (Coloss. 2:2), and to the Hebrews of the "full *assurance* of faith," and the "full *assurance* of hope"? (Heb. 6:11; 10:22)

♦ Does not Peter say expressly, "Give diligence to make your calling and election *sure*"? (2 Peter 1:10)

♦ Does not John say, "We *know* that we have passed from death unto life"? (1 John 3:14)

♦ And again, "These things have I written unto you that believe on the name of the Son of God, that ye may *know* that ye have eternal life." (1 John 5:13)

♦ And again, "We *know* that we are of God." (1 John 5:19)

Reader, what shall we say to these things? I desire to speak with all humility on any controverted point. I feel that I am only a poor fallible child of Adam myself. But I must say, that in the passages I have just quoted I see something far higher than the mere "hopes" and "trusts" with which so many believers appear content in this day. I see the language of persuasion, confidence, knowledge; nay, I may almost say, of certainty. And I feel, for my own part, if I may take these Scriptures in their plain, obvious meaning, the doctrine of assurance is true.

But my answer, furthermore, to all who dislike the doctrine of assurance, as bordering on presumption, is this: it can hardly be presumption to tread in the steps of Peter and Paul, of Job and of John. They were all eminently humble and lowly-minded men, if ever any were; and yet they all speak of their own state with an assured hope. Surely this should teach us that deep humility and strong assurance are perfectly compatible, and that there is not any necessary connection between spiritual confidence and pride.

My answer, furthermore, is, that many have attained to such an assured hope as our text expresses, even in modern times. I will not concede for a moment that it was a peculiar privilege confined to the Apostolic day. There have been, in our own land, many believers who have appeared to walk in almost uninterrupted fellowship with the Father and the Son, who have seemed to enjoy an almost unceasing sense of the light of God's reconciled countenance shining down upon them, and have left their experience on record. I could mention well-known names, if space permitted. The thing has been, and is, and that is enough.

My answer, lastly, is, it cannot be wrong to feel confidently in a matter where God speaks unconditionally, to believe decidedly when God promises decidedly, to have a sure persuasion of pardon and peace when we rest on the word and oath of Him that never changes. It is an utter mistake to suppose that the believer who feels assurance is resting on anything he sees in himself. He simply leans on the Mediator of the New Covenant, and the Scripture of truth. He believes the Lord Jesus means what He says, and takes Him at His Word. Assurance, after all, is no more than a full-grown faith; a masculine faith that grasps Christ's promise with both hands, a faith that argues like the good centurion, if the Lord "speak the word only," I am healed. Wherefore, then, should I doubt? (Matt. 8:8)

Reader, you may be sure that Paul was the last man in the world to build his assurance on anything of his own. He who could write himself down "chief of sinners" (1 Tim. 1:15) had a deep sense of his own guilt and corruption. But then he had a still deeper sense of the length and breadth of Christ's righteousness imputed to him. He, who would cry, "O wretched man that I am" (Rom. 7:24), had a clear view of the fountain of evil within his heart. But then he had a still clearer view of that other Fountain which can remove "all sin and uncleanness." He, who thought himself "less than the least of all saints" (Ephes. 3:8), had a lively and abiding feeling of his own weakness. But he had a still livelier feeling that Christ's promise, "My sheep shall never perish" (John 10:28), could not be broken; Paul knew, if ever man did, that he was a poor, frail bark, floating on a stormy ocean. He saw, if any did, the rolling waves and roaring tempest by which he was surrounded. But then he looked away from self to Jesus, and was not afraid. He remembered that anchor within the veil, which is both "sure and steadfast." He remembered the word, and work, and constant intercession of Him that loved him and gave Himself for him. And this it was, and nothing else, that enabled him to say so boldly, "A crown is laid up for me, and the Lord shall give it to me"; and to conclude so surely, "The Lord will preserve me: I shall never be confounded."

I may not dwell longer on this part of the subject. I think you will allow I have shown ground for the assertion I made; that assurance is a true thing.

II. *I PASS ON TO THE SECOND THING I SPOKE OF. I SAID, A BELIEVER MAY NEVER ARRIVE AT THIS ASSURED HOPE, WHICH PAUL EXPRESSES, AND YET BE SAVED.*

I grant this most freely. I do not dispute it for a moment. I would not desire to make one contrite heart sad that God has not made sad, or to discourage one fainting child of God, or to leave the impression that men have no part or lot in Christ, except they feel assurance. A person may have saving faith in Christ, and yet never enjoy an assured hope, like the Apostle Paul. To believe and have a glimmering hope of acceptance is one thing; to have joy and peace in our believing, and abound in hope, is quite another. All God's children have faith; not all have assurance. I think this ought never to be forgotten.

I know some great and good men have held a different opinion. I believe that many excellent ministers of the Gospel, at whose feet I would gladly sit, do not allow the distinction I have stated. But I desire to call no man master. I dread as much as anyone the idea of healing the wounds of conscience slightly; but I should think any other view than that I have given a most uncomfortable Gospel to preach, and one very likely to keep souls back a long time from the gate of life.

I do not shrink from saying, that by grace a man may have sufficient faith to flee to Christ; sufficient faith really to lay hold on Him, really to trust in Him, really to be a child of God, really to be saved; and yet to his last day be never free from much anxiety, doubt, and fear.

"A letter," says an old writer, "may be written, which is not sealed; so grace may be written in the heart, yet the Spirit may not set the seal of assurance to it." A child may be born heir to a great fortune, and yet never be aware of his riches; live childish, die childish, and never know the greatness of his possessions. And so also a man may be a babe in Christ's family; think as a babe, speak as a babe; and though saved, never enjoy a lively hope, or know the real privileges of his inheritance.

Reader, do not mistake my meaning, while you hear me dwell strongly on assurance. Do not do me the injustice to say, I told you none were saved except such as could say with Paul, "I know and am persuaded, there is a crown laid up for me." I do not say so. I tell you nothing of the kind. Faith in the Lord Jesus Christ a man must have, beyond all question, if he is to be saved. I know no other way of access to the Father. I see no intimation of mercy, excepting through Christ. A man must feel his sins and lost estate, must come to Jesus for pardon and salvation, must rest his hope on Him, and on Him alone. But if he only has faith to do this, however weak and feeble that faith may be, I will engage, from Scripture warrants, he shall not miss heaven.

Never, never let us curtail the freeness of the glorious Gospel, or clip its fair proportions. Never let us make the gate more strait and the way more narrow than pride and love of sin have made it already. The Lord Jesus is very pitiful, and of tender mercy. He does not regard the quantity of faith, but the quality. He does not measure its degree, but its truth. He will not break any bruised reed, nor quench any smoking flax. He will never let it be said that any perished at the foot of the cross. "Him that cometh unto Me," He says, "I will in no wise cast out." (John 6:37)

Yes, reader: though a man's faith be no bigger than a grain of mustard seed, if it only brings him to Christ, and enables him to touch the hem of His garment, he shall be saved, saved as surely as the oldest saint in paradise; saved as completely and eternally as Peter, or John, or Paul. There are degrees in our sanctification. In our justification there are none. What is written, is written, and shall never fail: "Whosoever believeth on Him," not whosoever has a strong and mighty faith, " Whosoever believeth on Him shall not be ashamed." (Rom. 10:11)

But all this time, I would have you take notice, the poor soul may have no full assurance of his pardon and acceptance with God. He may be troubled with fear upon fear, and doubt upon doubt. He may have many a question, and many an anxiety, many a struggle, and many a misgiving, clouds and darkness, storm and tempest to the very end.

I will engage, I repeat, that bare simple faith in Christ shall save a man, though he may never attain to assurance; but I will not engage it shall bring him to heaven with strong and abounding consolations. I will engage it shall land him safe in harbour; but I will not engage he shall enter that harbour in full sail, confident and rejoicing. I shall not be surprised if he reaches his desired haven weather-beaten and tempest-tossed, scarcely realizing his own safety, till he opens his eyes in glory.

We cannot come amiss to him that hath assurance: God is his. Hath he lost a friend? His Father lives. Hath he lost an only child? God hath given him His only Son. Hath he scarcity of bread? God hath given him the finest of the wheat, the bread of life. Are his comforts gone? He hath a Comforter. Doth he meet with storms? He knows where to put in for harbour. God is his portion, and heaven is his haven. - *Thomas Watson*

Full assurance is not essential to salvation, but it is essential to satisfaction. - *C.H. Spurgeon*

Assurance is glory in the bud, it is the suburbs of paradise.
- *Thomas Brooks*

Assurance is a most delicate plant. It needs daily, hourly, watering, tending, cherishing. So watch and pray the more when you have got it.
- *J.C. Ryle*

Is it necessary that men should be kept in continual dread of damnation, in order to render them circumspect and ensure their attention to duty? Will not the well-grounded expectation of heaven prove far more efficacious? Love is the noblest and strongest principle of obedience: nor can it be but that a sense of God's love to us will increase our desire to please Him. - *Thomas Robinson*

DAY 26

ASSURANCE – 2 TIM 4:6-8
BY J.C. RYLE
PART 2

READER, I BELIEVE IT IS OF great importance to keep in view this distinction between faith and assurance. It explains things which an inquirer in religion sometimes finds it hard to understand.

Faith, let us remember, is the root, and assurance is the flower. Doubtless, you can never have the flower without the root; but it is no less certain you may have the root and not the flower.

- ◆ *Faith* is that poor trembling woman who came behind Jesus in the press and touched the hem of His garment (Mark 5:27). *Assurance* is Stephen standing calmly in the midst of his murderers, and saying, "I see the heavens opened, and the Son of man standing on the right hand of God!"

- ◆ *Faith* is the penitent thief, crying, "Lord, remember me" (Luke 23:42). *Assurance* is Job, sitting in the dust, covered with sores, and saying, "I know that my Redeemer liveth" (Job 19:25). "Though He slay me, yet will I trust in Him" (Job 13:15).

- ◆ *Faith* is Peter's drowning cry, as he began to sink: "Lord, save me" (Matt 14:30). *Assurance* is that same Peter declaring before the Council in after times, "This is the stone which was set at nought of you builders, which is become the head of the corner. Neither is there salvation in any other; for there is none other name under heaven given among men, whereby we must be saved" (Acts 4:11-12).

- ◆ *Faith* is the anxious, trembling voice, "Lord, I believe; help Thou mine unbelief" (Mark 9:24). *Assurance* is the confident challenge, "Who shall lay anything to the charge of God's elect? . . . Who is he that condemneth?" (Rom 8:33, 34).

- ◆ *Faith* is Saul praying in the house of Judas at Damascus, sorrowful, blind, and alone (Acts 9:11). *Assurance* is Paul, the aged prisoner, looking calmly into the grave, and saying, "I know whom I have believed… There is a crown laid up for me" (2 Tim 1:12, 4:8).

Faith is life: How great the blessing! Who can tell the gulf between life and death? And yet life may be weak, sickly, unhealthy, painful, trying, anxious, worn, burdensome, joyless, smileless to the very end. Assurance is more than life: It is health, strength, power, vigor, activity, energy, manliness, beauty.

Reader, it is not a question of saved or not saved that lies before us, but of privilege or no privilege. It is not a question of peace or no peace, but of great peace or little peace. It is not a question between the wanderers of this world and the school of Christ: it is one that belongs only to the school: it is between the first form and the last.

He that has faith does well. Happy should I be, if I thought all readers of this article had it. Blessed, thrice blessed are they that believe. They are safe. They are washed. They are justified. They are beyond the power of hell. Satan, with all his malice, shall never pluck them out of Christ's hand. But he that has assurance does far better, sees more, feels more, knows more, enjoys more, has more days like those spoken of in Deuteronomy 11:21, even "as the days of heaven upon the earth."

III. I PASS ON TO THE THIRD THING OF WHICH I SPOKE. I WILL GIVE YOU SOME REASONS WHY AN ASSURED HOPE IS EXCEEDINGLY TO BE DESIRED.

I ask your attention to this point especially. I heartily wish that assurance was more sought after than it is. Too many among those who believe begin doubting and go on doubting, live doubting and die doubting, and go to heaven in a kind of mist.

It will ill become me to speak in a slighting way of "hopes" and "trusts." But I fear many of us sit down content with them, and go no farther. I should like to see fewer "peradventurers" in the Lord's family, and more who could say, "I know and am persuaded." Oh, that all believers would covet the best gifts, and not be content with less! Many miss the full tide of blessedness the Gospel was meant to convey. Many keep themselves in a low and starved condition of soul, while their Lord is saying, "Eat and drink abundantly, O beloved. Ask and receive, that your joy may be full." (Cant. 5:1, John 16:24)

1. Let us remember, then, for one thing, that assurance is to be desired, because of the present comfort and peace it affords.

Doubts and fears have power to spoil much of the happiness of a true believer in Christ. Uncertainty and suspense are bad enough in any condition, in the matter of our health, our property, our families, our affections, our earthly callings, but never so bad as in the affairs of our souls. And so long as a believer cannot get beyond "I hope" and "I trust," he manifestly feels a degree of uncertainty about his spiritual state. The very words imply as much. He says, "I hope," because he dares not say, "I know."

Now assurance goes far to set a child of God free from this painful kind of bondage, and thus ministers mightily to his comfort. It enables him to feel that the great business of life is a settled business, the great debt a paid debt, the great disease a healed disease, and the great work a finished work; and all other business, diseases, debts, and works, are then by comparison small. In this way assurance makes him patient in tribulation, calm under bereavements, unmoved in sorrow, not afraid of evil tidings; in every condition content, for it gives him a fixedness of heart. It sweetens his bitter cups, it lessens the burden of his crosses, it smoothes the rough places over which he travels, and it lightens the valley of the shadow of death. It makes him always feel that he has something solid beneath his feet, and something firm under his hands, a sure friend by the way, and a sure home at the end.

♦ Assurance will help a man to bear poverty and loss. It will teach him to say, "I know that I have in heaven a better and more enduring substance. Silver and gold have I none, but grace and glory are mine, and these can never make themselves wings and flee away. Though the fig tree shall not blossom, yet I will rejoice in the Lord." (Habakkuk 3:17-18)

♦ Assurance will support a child of God under the heaviest bereavements, and assist him to feel "It is well." An assured soul will say, "Though beloved ones are taken from me, yet Jesus is the same, and is alive for evermore. Though my house be not as flesh and blood could wish, yet I have an everlasting covenant, ordered in all things and sure." (2 Kings 4:26, Heb. 13:8, 2 Sam. 23:5)

♦ Assurance will enable a man to praise God, and be thankful, even in a prison, like Paul and Silas at Philippi. It can give a believer songs even in the darkest night, and joy when all things seem going against him. (Job 21:10, Psalm 42:8)

♦ Assurance will enable a man to sleep with the full prospect of death on the morrow, like Peter in Herod's dungeon. It will teach him to say, "I will both lay me down in peace and sleep, for thou, Lord, only makest me to dwell in safety." (Psalm 4:8)

♦ Assurance can make a man rejoice to suffer shame for Christ's sake, as the Apostles did. It will remind him that he may "rejoice and be exceeding glad" (Matt. 5:12), and that there is in heaven an exceeding weight of glory that shall make amends for all. (2 Cor. 4:17)

♦ Assurance will enable a believer to meet a violent and painful death without fear, as Stephen did in the beginning of Christ's Church, and as Cranmer, Ridley, Latimer, and Taylor did in our own land. It will bring to his heart the texts, "Be not afraid of them which kill the body, and after that have no more that they can do." (Luke 12:4) "Lord Jesus receive my spirit." (Acts 7:59)

◆ Assurance will support a man in pain and sickness, make all his bed, smooth down his dying pillow. It will enable him to say, "If my earthly house fail, I have a building of God." (2 Cor. 5:1) "I desire to depart and be with Christ." (Phil. 1:23) "My flesh and my heart may fail, but God is the strength of my heart, and my portion forever." (Psalm 73:26)

Reader, the comfort assurance can give in the hour of death is a point of great importance. Believe me, you will never think assurance so precious as when your turn comes to die. In that awful hour, there are few believers who do not find out the value and privilege of an "assured hope," whatever they may have thought about it during their lives. General "hopes" and "trusts" are all very well to live upon, while the sun shines, and the body is strong: but when you come to die, you will want to be able to say, "I know" and "I feel." Believe me, Jordan is a cold stream, and we have to cross it alone. No earthly friend can help us. The last enemy, even death, is a strong foe. When our souls are departing there is no cordial like the strong wine of assurance.

There is a beautiful expression in the Prayer-book service for the Visitation of the Sick: "The Almighty Lord, who is a most strong tower to all them that put their trust in Him, be now and evermore thy defense, and make thee know and feel that there is none other name under heaven, through whom thou mayest receive health and salvation, but only the name of our Lord Jesus Christ." The compilers of that service showed great wisdom there. They saw that when the eyes grow dim, and the heart grows faint, and the spirit is on the eve of departing, there must then be knowing and feeling what Christ has done for us, or else there cannot be perfect peace.

2. Let us remember, for another thing, that assurance is to be desired, because it tends to make a Christian an active working Christian.

None, generally speaking, do so much for Christ on earth as those who enjoy the fullest confidence of a free entrance into heaven. That sounds wonderful, I dare say, but it is true. A believer who lacks an assured hope will spend much of his time in inward searchings of heart about his own state. Like a nervous, hypochondriacal person, he will be full of his own ailments, his own doubtings and questionings, his own conflicts and corruptions. In short, you will often find he is so taken up with this internal warfare that he has little leisure for other things, little time to work for God.

Now a believer, who has, like Paul, an assured hope, is free from these harassing distractions. He does not vex his soul with doubts about his own pardon and acceptance. He looks at the everlasting covenant sealed with blood, at the finished work and never-broken word of his Lord and Saviour, and therefore counts his salvation a settled thing. And thus he is able to give an undivided attention to the work of the Lord, and so in the long run to do more.

Take, for an illustration of this, two English emigrants, and suppose them set down side by side in New Zealand or Australia. Give each of them a piece of land to clear and cultivate. Let the portions allotted to them be the same both in quantity and quality. Secure that land to them by every needful legal instrument; let it be conveyed as freehold to them and theirs forever; let the conveyance be publicly registered, and the property made sure to them by every deed and security that man's ingenuity can devise.

Suppose, then, that one of them shall set to work to bring his land into cultivation, and labour at it day after day without intermission or cessation. Suppose, in the meanwhile, that the other shall be continually leaving his work, and going repeatedly to the public registry to ask whether the land really is his own, whether there is not some mistake, whether, after all, there is not some flaw in the legal instruments which conveyed it to him. The one shall never doubt his title, but just work diligently on. The other shall hardly ever feel sure of his title, and spend half his time in going to Sydney, or Melbourne, or Auckland with needless inquiries about it.

Which, now, of these two men will have made most progress in a year's time? Who will have done the most for his land, got the greatest breadth of soil under tillage, have the best crops to show, be altogether the most prosperous? Reader, you know as well as I do. I need not supply an answer. There can only be one reply. Undivided attention will always attain the greatest success.

It is much the same in the matter of our title to "mansions in the skies." None will do so much for the Lord who bought him as the believer who sees his title clear, and is not distracted by unbelieving hesitations. The joy of the Lord will be that man's strength. "Restore unto me," says David, "the joy of Thy salvation; then will I teach transgressors Thy ways." (Psalm 51:12) Never were there such working Christians as the Apostles. They seemed to live to labour. Christ's work was truly their meat and drink. They counted not their lives dear to themselves. They spent and were spent. They laid down ease, health, and worldly comfort, at the foot of the cross. And one grand cause of this, I believe, was their assured hope. They were men who could say, "We know that we are of God, and the whole world lieth in wickedness." (1 John 5:19)

3. Let us remember, for another thing, that assurance is to be desired, because it tends to make a Christian a decided Christian.

Indecision and doubt about our own state in God's sight is a grievous one, and the mother of many evils. It often produces a wavering and unstable walk in following the Lord. Assurance helps to cut many a knot, and to make the path of Christian duty clear and plain.

Many, of whom we feel hopes that they are God's children, and have true grace, however weak, are continually perplexed with doubts on points of practice. "Should we do such and such a thing? Shall we give up this family custom? Ought we to go into that company? How shall we draw the line about visiting? What is to be the measure of our dressing and our entertainments? Are we never, under any circumstances, to dance, never to touch a card, never to attend parties of pleasure?" These are a kind of questions which seem to give them constant trouble. And often, very often, the simple root of their perplexity is, that they do not feel assured they are themselves children of God. They have not yet settled the point, which side of the gate they are on. They do not know whether they are inside the ark or not.

That a child of God ought to act in a certain decided way they quite feel, but the grand question is, "Are they children of God themselves?" If they only felt they were so, they would go straightforward, and take a decided line. But not feeling sure about it, their conscience is forever hesitating and coming to a dead lock. The devil whispers, "Perhaps, after all, you are only a hypocrite: what right have you to take a decided course? Wait till you are really a Christian." And this whisper too often turns the scale, and leads on to some miserable compromise, or wretched conformity to the world.

Reader, I believe you have here one chief reason why so many in this day are inconsistent, trimming, unsatisfactory, and half-hearted in their conduct about the world. Their faith fails. They feel no assurance that they are Christ's, and so feel a hesitancy about breaking with the world. They shrink from laying aside all the ways of the old man, because they are not quite confident they have put on the new. Depend on it, one secret cause of halting between two opinions is want of assurance. When people can say decidedly, "The Lord He is the God," their course becomes very clear. (1 Kings 18:39)

IV.   LET US REMEMBER, FINALLY, THAT ASSURANCE IS TO BE DESIRED, BECAUSE IT TENDS TO MAKE THE HOLIEST CHRISTIANS.

This, too, sounds wonderful and strange, and yet it is true. It is one of the paradoxes of the Gospel, contrary, at first sight, to reason and common sense, and yet it to a fact. Cardinal Bellarmine was seldom more wide of the truth than when he said, "Assurance tends to carelessness and sloth." He that is freely forgiven by Christ will always do much for Christ's glory, and he that enjoys the fullest assurance of this forgiveness will ordinarily keep up the closest walk with God. It is a faithful saying in 1 John 3:3 - "He that hath this hope in Him purifieth himself even as He is pure." A hope that does not purify is a mockery, a delusion, and a snare.

None are so likely to maintain a watchful guard over hearts and lives as those who know the comfort of living in near communion with God. They feel their privilege, and will fear losing it. They will dread falling from their high estate, and marring their own comforts, by bringing clouds between themselves and Christ. He that goes on a journey with little money about him takes little thought of danger, and cares little how late he travels. He, on the contrary, that carries gold and jewels will be a cautious traveller. He will look well to his roads, his house, and his company, and run no risks. The fixed stars are those that tremble most. The man that most fully enjoys the light of God's reconciled countenance, will be a man tremblingly afraid of losing its blessed consolations, and jealously fearful of doing anything to grieve the Holy Ghost.

Reader, I commend these four points to your serious consideration. Would you like to feel the everlasting arms around you, and to hear the voice of Jesus daily drawing nigh to your soul, and saying, "I am thy salvation"? Would you like to be a useful labourer in the vineyard in your day and generation? Would you be known of all men as a bold, firm, decided, single-eyed, uncompromising follower of Christ? Would you be eminently spiritually-minded and holy? I doubt not some readers will say, "These are the very things our hearts desire. We long for them. We pant after them: but they seem far from us."

Assurance is optimum maximum, the best and greatest mercy; and therefore God will only give it to his best and dearest friends.
- *Thomas Brooks*

Are you in depths and doubts, staggering and uncertain, not knowing what is your condition, nor whether you have any interest in the forgiveness that is of God? Are you tossed up and down between hopes and fears, and want peace consolation, and establishment? Why lie you upon your faces? Get up: watch, pray, fast, meditate, offer violence to your lusts and corruptions; fear not, startle not at their crying to be spared; press unto the throne of grace by prayer, supplications, importunities, restless requests: this is the way to take the kingdom of God. These things are not peace, are not assurance; but they are part of the means God hath appointed for the attainment of them. - *John Owen*

Whenever God pardons sin, He subdues it, Micah 7:19. Then is the condemning power of sin taken away, when the commanding power of it is taken away. If a malefactor be in prison, how shall he know that his prince hath pardoned him? If a jailer come and knock off his chains and fetters, and lets him out of prison, then he may know he is pardoned; so, how shall we know God hath pardoned us? If the fetters of sin be broken off, and we walk at liberty in the ways of God, this is a blessed sign we are pardoned. - *Thomas Watson*

What a support to our faith is this, that God the Father, the party offended by our sins, is so well pleased with the work of redemption!
- *Richard Sibbes*

Many a Christian has his pardon sealed in the court of heaven before it is sealed in the court of his own conscience. - *Thomas Brooks*

DAY 27

ASSURANCE – 2 TIM 4:6-8
BY J.C. RYLE
PART 3

NOW, HAS IT NEVER struck you that your neglect of assurance may possibly be the main secret of all your failures, that the low measure of faith which satisfies you may be the cause of your low degree of peace? Can you think it a strange thing that your graces are faint and languishing, when faith, the root and mother of them all, is allowed to remain feeble and weak?

Take my advice this day. Seek an increase of faith. Seek an assured hope of salvation like the Apostle Paul's. Seek to obtain a simple, childlike confidence in God's promises. Seek to be able to say with Paul, "I know whom I have believed: I am persuaded that He is mine, and I am His." You have very likely tried other ways and methods and completely failed. Change your plan. Go upon another tack. Lay aside your doubts. Lean more entirely on the Lord's arm. Begin with implicit trusting. Cast aside your faithless backwardness to take the Lord at His word. Come and roll yourself, your soul, and your sins upon your gracious Saviour. Begin with simple believing, and all other things shall soon be added to you.

V. *I COME NOW TO THE LAST THING OF WHICH I SPOKE. I PROMISED TO POINT OUT TO YOU SOME PROBABLE CAUSES WHY AN ASSURED HOPE IS SO SELDOM ATTAINED. I WILL DO IT VERY SHORTLY.*

This is a very serious question, and ought to raise in all great searchings of heart. Few, certainly, of Christ's people seem to reach up to this blessed spirit of assurance. Many comparatively believe, but few are persuaded. Many comparatively have saving faith, but few that glorious confidence which shines forth in the language of St. Paul. That such is the case, I think we must all allow.

Now, why is this so? Why is a thing which two Apostles have strongly enjoined us to seek after, a thing of which few believers have any experimental knowledge? Why is an assured hope so rare? I desire to offer a few suggestions on this point, with all humility. I know that many have never attained assurance, at whose feet I would gladly sit both in earth and heaven. Perhaps the Lord sees something in the natural temperament of some of His children, which makes assurance not good for them. Perhaps, in order to be kept in spiritual health, they need to be kept very low. God only knows. Still, after every allowance, I fear there are many believers without an assured hope, whose case may too often be explained by causes such as these.

1. One most common cause, I suspect, is a defective view of the doctrine of justification.

I am inclined to think that justification and sanctification are insensibly confused together in the minds of many believers. They receive the Gospel truth, that there must be something done IN US, as well as something done FOR US, if we are true members of Christ; and so far they are right. But, then, without being aware of it, perhaps, they seem to imbibe the idea that their justification is, in some degree, affected by something within themselves. They do not clearly see that Christ's work, not their own work, either in whole or in part, either directly or indirectly, is the alone ground of our acceptance with God; that justification is a thing entirely without us, for which nothing whatever is needful on our part but simple faith, and that the weakest believer is as fully and completely justified as the strongest.

Many appear to forget that we are saved and justified as sinners, and only sinners; and that we never can attain to anything higher, if we live to the age of Methuselah. Redeemed sinners, justified sinners, and renewed sinners doubtless we must be; but sinners, sinners, sinners, always to the very last. They do not seem to comprehend that there is a wide difference between our justification and our sanctification. Our justification is a perfect finished work, and admits of no degrees. Our sanctification is imperfect and incomplete, and will be to the last hour of our life. They appear to expect that a believer may at some period of his life be in a measure free from corruption, and attain to a kind of inward perfection. And not finding this angelic state of things in their own hearts, they at once conclude there must be something very wrong in their state. And so they go mourning all their days; oppressed with fears that they have no part or lot in Christ, and refusing to be comforted.

Reader, consider this point well. If any believing soul desires assurance, and has not got it, let him ask himself, first of all, if he is quite sure he is sound in the faith, if his loins are thoroughly "girt about with truth," and his eyes thoroughly clear in the matter of justification. He must know what it is simply to believe before he can expect to feel assured.

Believe me, the old Galatian heresy is the most fertile source of error, both in doctrine and in practice. Seek clearer views of Christ, and what Christ has done for you. Happy is the man who really understands justification by faith without the deeds of the law.

2. Another common cause of the absence of assurance is, slothfulness about growth in grace.

I suspect many true believers hold dangerous and unscriptural views on this point: I do not of course mean intentionally, but they do hold them. Many appear to me to think that once converted, they have little more to attend to, and that a state of salvation is a kind of easy chair, in which they may just sit still, lie back, and be happy. They seem to fancy that grace is given them that they may enjoy it, and they forget that it is given, like a talent, to be used, employed, and improved. Such persons lose sight of the many direct injunctions "to increase, to grow, to abound more and more, to add to our faith," and the like; and in this little-doing condition, this sitting-still state of mind, I never marvel that they miss assurance.

I believe it ought to be our continual aim and desire to go forward; and our watchword at the beginning of every year should be, "More and more" (1 Thess. 4:1): more knowledge, more faith, more obedience, more love. If we have brought forth thirty-fold, we should seek to bring forth sixty, and if we have brought forth sixty, we should strive to bring forth a hundred. The will of the Lord is our sanctification, and it ought to be our will too. (Matt. 13:23, 1 Thess. 4:3)

One thing, at all events, we may depend upon, there is an inseparable connection between diligence and assurance. "Give diligence," says Peter, "to make your calling and election sure." (2 Peter 1:10) "We desire," says Paul, "that every one of you do show the same diligence to the full assurance of hope unto the end." (Heb. 6:11) "The soul of the diligent," says Solomon, "shall be made fat." (Prov. 13:4) There is much truth in the old maxim of the Puritans: "Faith of adherence comes by hearing, but faith of assurance comes not without doing."

Reader, mark my words. Are you one of those who desires assurance, but have not got it? You will never get it without diligence, however much you may desire it. There are no gains without pains in spiritual things, any more than in temporal. "The soul of the sluggard desireth and hath nothing." (Prov. 13:4)

3. Another common cause of a want of assurance is, an inconsistent walk in life.

With grief and sorrow I feel constrained to say, I fear nothing in this day more frequently prevents men attaining an assured hope than this. The stream of professing Christianity is far wider than it formerly was, and I am afraid we must admit, at the same time, it is much less deep.

Inconsistency of life is utterly destructive of peace of conscience. The two things are incompatible. They cannot and they will not go together. If you will have your besetting sins, and cannot make up your minds to give them up; if you will shrink from cutting off the right hand and plucking out the right eye, when occasion requires it, I will engage you will have no assurance. A vacillating walk, a backwardness to take a bold and decided line, a readiness to conform to the world, a hesitating witness for Christ, a lingering tone of religion; all these make up a sure receipt for bringing a blight upon the garden of your soul.

It is vain to suppose you will feel assured and persuaded of your own pardon and acceptance with God, unless you count all God's commandments concerning all things to be right, and hate every sin, whether great or small. (Psalm 119:128) One Achan allowed in the camp of your heart will weaken your hands, and lay your consolations low in the dust. You must be daily sowing to the Spirit, if you are to reap the witness of the Spirit. You will not find and feel that all the Lord's ways are ways of pleasantness, unless you labour in all your ways to please the Lord.

I bless God our salvation in no wise depends on our own works. By grace we are saved, not by works of righteousness, through faith, without the deeds of the law. But I never would have any believer for a moment forget that our sense of salvation depends much on the manner of our living. Inconsistency will dim your eyes, and bring clouds between you and the sun. The sun is the same behind the clouds, but you will not be able to see its brightness or enjoy its warmth, and your soul will be gloomy and cold. It is in the path of well doing that the day-spring of assurance will visit you, and shine down upon your heart.

"The secret of the Lord," says David, "is with them that fear Him, and He will show them His covenant." - Psalm 25:14

To him that ordereth his conversation aright will I shew the salvation of God. - Psalm 50:23

Great peace have they which love Thy law, and nothing shall offend them. - Psalm 119:165

If we walk in the light, as He is in the light, we have fellowship one with an-other. - 1 John 1:7

Let us not love in word, neither in tongue; but in deed and in truth. And hereby we know that we are of the truth, and shall assure our hearts before Him. - 1 John 3:18-19

Hereby we do know that we know Him, if we keep His commandments. - 1 John 2:3

Paul was a man who exercised himself to have always a conscience void of offence toward God and toward man. (Acts 24:16) He could say with boldness, "I have fought the good fight, I have kept the faith." I do not wonder that the Lord enabled him to add with confidence, "Henceforth there is a crown laid up for me, and the Lord shall give it me at that day."

Reader, if any believer in the Lord Jesus desires assurance, and has not got it, let him think over this point also. Let him look at his own heart, look at his own conscience, look at his own life, look at his own ways, look at his own home. And perhaps when he has done that, he will be able to say, "There is a cause why I have no assured hope." I leave the three matters I have just mentioned to your own private consideration. I am sure they are worth examining. May you examine them honestly. And may the Lord give you understanding in all things.

AND NOW, IN CLOSING THIS IMPORTANT INQUIRY: let me speak first to those readers who have not given themselves to the Lord, who have not yet come out from the world, chosen the good part, and followed Christ. I ask you, then, to learn from this subject the privileges and comforts of a true Christian.

I would not have you judge of the Lord Jesus Christ by His people. The best of servants can give you but a faint idea of that glorious Master. Neither would I have you judge of the privileges of His kingdom by the measure of comfort to which many of His people attain. Alas, we are most of us poor creatures! We come short, very short, of the blessedness we might enjoy. But, depend upon it, there are glorious things in the city of our God, which they who have an assured hope taste, even in their life-time. There are lengths and breadths of peace and consolation there, which it has not entered into your heart to conceive. There is bread enough and to spare in our Father's house, though many of us certainly eat but little of it, and continue weak. But the fault must not be laid to our Master's charge: it is all our own.

And, after all, the weakest child of God has a mine of comforts within him, of which you know nothing. You see the conflicts and tossings of the surface of his heart, but you see not the pearls of great price which are hidden in the depths below. The feeblest member of Christ would not change conditions with you. The believer who possesses the least assurance is far better off than you are. He has a hope, however faint, but you have none at all. He has a portion that will never be taken from him, a Saviour that will never forsake him, a treasure that fadeth not away, however little he may realize it all at present. But, as for you, if you die as you are, your expectations will all perish. Oh, that you were wise! Oh, that you understood these things! Oh, that you would consider your latter end!

I feel deeply for you in these latter days of the world, if I ever did. I feel deeply for those whose treasure is all on earth, and whose hopes are all on this side the grave. Yes: when I see old kingdoms and dynasties shaking to the very foundation, when I see, as we all saw a few years ago, kings, and princes, and rich men, and great men fleeing for their lives, and scarce knowing where to hide their heads, when I see property dependent on public confidence melting like snow in spring, and public stocks and funds losing their value, when I see these things I feel deeply for those who have no better portion than this world can give them, and no place in that kingdom that cannot be removed.

Take advice of a minister of Christ this very day. Seek durable riches, a treasure that cannot be taken from you, a city which hath lasting foundations. Do as the Apostle Paul did. Give yourself to the Lord Jesus Christ, and seek that incorruptible crown He is ready to bestow. Take His yoke upon you, and learn of Him. Come away from a world which will never really satisfy you, and from sin which will bite like a serpent if you cling to it, at last. Come to the Lord Jesus as lowly sinners, and He will receive you, pardon you, give you His renewing Spirit, fill you with peace. This shall give you more real comfort than the world has ever done. There is a gulf in your heart which nothing but the peace of Christ can fill. Enter in and share our privileges. Come with us, and sit down by our side.

LASTLY: let me turn to all believers who read these pages, and speak to them a few words of brotherly counsel. The main thing that I urge upon you is this; if you have not got an assured hope of your own acceptance in Christ, resolve this day to seek it. Labour for it. Strive after it. Pray for it. Give the Lord no rest till you "know whom you have believed."

I feel, indeed, that the small amount of assurance in this day, among those who are reckoned God's children, is a shame and a reproach. "It is a thing to be heavily bewailed," says old Traill, "that many Christians have lived twenty or forty years since Christ called them by His grace, yet doubting in their life." Let us call to mind the earnest "desire" Paul expresses, that "everyone" of the Hebrews should seek after full assurance and let us endeavour, by God's blessing, to roll this reproach away. (Heb. 6:11)

Believing reader, do you really mean to say that you have no desire to exchange hope for confidence, trust for persuasion, uncertainty for knowledge? Because weak faith will save you, will you therefore rest content with it? Because assurance is not essential to your entrance into heaven, will you therefore be satisfied without it upon earth? Alas, this is not a healthy state of soul to be in; this is not the mind of the Apostolic day! Arise at once, and go forward. Stick not at the foundations of religion: go on to perfection. Be not content with a day of small things. Never despise it in others, but never be content with it yourselves.

Believe me, believe me, assurance is worth the seeking. You forsake your own mercies when you rest content without it. The things I speak are for your peace. If it is good to be sure in earthly things, how much better is it to be sure in heavenly things. Your salvation is a fixed and certain thing. God knows it. Why should not you seek to know it too? There is nothing unscriptural in this. Paul never saw the book of life, and yet Paul says, "I know, and am persuaded."

Make it, then, your daily prayer that you may have an increase of faith. According to your faith will be your peace. Cultivate that blessed root more, and sooner or later, by God's blessing, you may hope to have the flower, You may not, perhaps, attain to full assurance all at once. It is good sometimes to be kept waiting. We do not value things which we get without trouble. But though it tarry, wait for it. Seek on, and expect to find.

There is one thing, however, of which I would not have you ignorant: you must not be surprised if you have occasional doubts after you have got assurance.

You must not forget you are on earth, and not yet in heaven. You are still in the body, and have indwelling sin: the flesh will lust against the spirit to the very end. The leprosy will never be out of the walls of the old house till death takes it down. And there is a devil, too, and a strong devil: a devil who tempted the Lord Jesus, and gave Peter a fall; and he will take care you know it. Some doubts there always will be. He that never doubts has nothing to lose. He that never fears possesses nothing truly valuable. He that is never jealous knows little of deep love. But be not discouraged: you shall be more than conquerors through Him that loved you.

Finally, do not forget that assurance is a thing that may be lost for a season, even by the brightest Christians, unless they take care. Assurance is a most delicate plant. It needs daily, hourly watching, watering, tending, cherishing. So watch and pray the more when you have got it. As Rutherford says, "Make much of assurance." Be always upon your guard. When Christian slept, in *Pilgrim's Progress*, he lost his certificate. Keep that in mind.

David lost assurance for many months by falling into transgression. Peter lost it when he denied his Lord. Each found it again, undoubtedly, but not till after bitter tears. Spiritual darkness comes on horseback, and goes away on foot. It is upon us before we know that it is coming. It leaves us slowly, gradually, and not till after many days. It is easy to run downhill. It is hard work to climb up. So remember my caution, when you have the joy of the Lord, watch and pray.

Above all, grieve not the Spirit. Quench not the Spirit. Vex not the Spirit. Drive Him not to a distance, by tampering with small bad habits and little sins. Little jarrings between husbands and wives make unhappy homes, and petty inconsistencies, known and allowed, will bring in a strangeness between you and the Spirit.

HEAR THE CONCLUSION OF THE WHOLE MATTER: The man who walks with God in Christ most closely will generally be kept in the greatest peace. The believer who follows the Lord most fully will ordinarily enjoy the most assured hope, and have the clearest persuasion of his own salvation.

The more the soul is conformed to Christ, the more confident it will be of its interest in Christ. - *Thomas Brooks*

See here, for our comfort, a sweet agreement of all three persons: the Father giveth a commission to Christ; the Spirit furnisheth and sanctifieth to it; Christ himself executeth the office of a Mediator. Our redemption is founded upon the joint agreement of all three persons of the Trinity. - *Richard Sibbes*

The believer who follows the Lord most fully will ordinarily enjoy the most assured hope! - *J C. Ryle*

No believer should be content with hoping and trusting, he should ask the Lord to lead him on to full assurance, so that matters of hope may become matters
of certainty. - *C.H. Spurgeon*

Assurance would make us active and lively in God's service; it would excite prayer, quicken obedience. Faith would make us walk, but assurance would make us run; we should think we could never do enough for God. Assurance would be as wings to the bird, as weights to the clock, to set all the wheels of obedience a-running. - *Thomas Watson*

DAY 28

THE GREAT SHEPHERD
BY JOHN NEWTON

He will feed His flock like a shepherd. He will carry the lambs in His arms, holding them close to His heart. He will gently lead the mother sheep with their young.
- Isaiah 40:11

OUR LORD EXPRESSLY calls Himself the "good Shepherd of the sheep", and the apostle Peter calls Him the "chief Shepherd." (John 10, 1 Peter 5:4) With respect to power and authority, He is the chief, and, indeed, the sole Shepherd. The eyes of all His people are upon Him and His watchful eye is upon and over all His flock. None but an omnipotent and omnipresent Shepherd can relieve all the necessities of all of His people, in all places, in the same moment, and be equally near and attentive to each one! Such is our great Shepherd! He is eminently the good Shepherd also, for He laid down His life for His sheep, and has redeemed them by His own blood.

This great and good Shepherd has a flock, whom He loved from eternity, and whom having once loved, He will love them to the end! (John 13:1) He humbled Himself for their sakes, submitted to partake of their nature and their sorrows, and was made in the likeness of sinful flesh. He died for His sheep, "the just for the unjust," to redeem them from the curse of the law, from the guilt and dominion of sin, from the power of Satan, and to bring them to God!

They all, by nature, had "gone astray, everyone to his own way;" but having thus bought them with His blood, in His own appointed time, He seeks, finds and restores His sheep! By the power of His Word and Spirit, He makes Himself known to their hearts, causes them to hear and understand His voice, and guides them into His fold! They are then under His immediate protection and government.

Considered as individuals, they are fitly described by the name of "sheep". A sheep is a weak, defenseless, foolish creature; prone to wander, and can seldom return of its own accord. A sheep has neither strength to fight with the wolf, nor speed to escape from it; nor has a sheep the foresight of the ant, to provide its own sustenance.

SUCH IS OUR CHARACTER, AND OUR SITUATION! WE ARE:

- Unable to take care of ourselves
- Prone to wander from our resting-place
- Exposed to enemies which we can neither escape nor withstand
- Without any resource in ourselves
- Taught, by daily experience, the insufficiency of everything around us

Yet, if Jesus is our Shepherd, as weak and helpless as we are, we may say with David, "The Lord is my Shepherd, I have everything I need! Surely Your goodness and unfailing love will pursue me all the days of my life, and I will live in the house of the Lord forever!" Every sheep has an inheritance reserved for them in heaven, (1 Peter 1:4-5) and they shall be safely kept, while they are sojourners upon earth, for the Shepherd of Israel is their keeper.

The Good Shepherd cares for His flock. Not the slightest circumstance in their concerns, escapes His notice. When they are ready to faint, borne down with heavy exercises of mind, wearied with temptations, dry and disconsolate in their hearts; He seasonably revives them. Nor are they in affliction without a needs-be for it. All His dispensations towards them are medicinal, designed to correct, or to restrain, or to cure, the maladies of their souls. And they are all adjusted, by His wisdom and tenderness, to what they can bear, and to what their case requires. The Good Shepherd is represented as counting their sighs, putting their tears into His bottle, recording their sorrows in His book of remembrance; and as being "able to sympathize with our weaknesses."

There are lambs among His flock, and for these He expresses a special tenderness. "He will carry the lambs in His arms, holding them close to His heart." Though they are weaklings, they shall not be left behind. If a poor lamb is weary, and unable to keep up with the flock, He shall carry it. These are new converts in the Lord's family; they are, as yet, weak, unsettled and inexperienced. Almost every day brings them into a new and untried situation. They often meet with opposition and discouragement. What would become of them in such circumstances, if their faithful Shepherd had not promised that "He will carry the lambs in His arms, holding them close to His heart!"

Assurance will make a man fervent, constant, and abundant in the work of the Lord. When the assured Christian hath done one work, he is calling out for another. What is next, Lord, says the assured soul, what is next? An assured Christian will put his hand to any work, he will put his neck in any yoke for Christ - he never thinks he hath done enough, he always thinks he had done too little; and when he hath done all he can, he sits down, saying, I am an unprofitable servant. - *Thomas Brooks*

The plow goes before the seed be sown; the heart must be plowed up by humiliation and repentance, before God sows the seed of assurance.
- *Thomas Watson*

Who is more obliged, or who feels the obligation to observance more cogently - the son who knows his near relation, and knows his father loves him, or the servant that hath great reason to doubt it? Fear is a weak and impotent principle in comparison of love. Terrors may awaken; love enlivens. Terrors may "almost persuade;" love over-persuades. Sure am I that a believer's knowledge that his Beloved is his, and he is his Beloved's (Cant. vi. 3), is found by experience to lay the most strong and cogent obligations upon him to loyalty and faithfulness to the Lord Jesus. For as to him that believes Christ is precious (1 Peter ii. 7), so to him that knows he believes Christ is so much the more precious, even the "chiefest of ten thousand." (Cant. v. 10)
- *Richard Fairclough*

A lazy Christian shall always want (lack) four things: comfort, content, confidence, and assurance. God hath made a separation between joy and idleness, between assurance and laziness; and, therefore, it is impossible for thee to bring these together that God hath put so far asunder.
- *Thomas Brooks*

Faith will make us walk, but assurance will make us run. - *Thomas Watson*

DAY 29

ASSURANCE OF SALVATION
BY HORATIUS BONAR
PART 1

"CHRIST FOR US," the obedient in the place of the disobedient, is the first part of our message. His assumption of the legal claims, which otherwise would have been made good against us, is the security for our deliverance. That deliverance becomes an actual thing to us immediately upon our consenting to allow him to undertake our case.

"Christ in us" is the second part of our Gospel. This second is of mighty moment, and yet is not to be confounded with the first. That which is done for us is not the same as that which is done in us. By the former we are constituted righteous, by the latter we are made holy. The one is properly the Gospel, in the belief of which we are saved; the other, the carrying out of that Gospel in the soul. Christ "for us" is our justification. "Christ in us, and we in Christ," is our holiness. The former is the external substitution; the latter, the internal energy or operation, taking its rise from the former, yet not to be confounded with it, or substituted for it. Christ the substitute, giving his life for ours upon the cross, is specially the object of faith. The message concerning this sacrificial work is the Gospel, the belief which brings pardon to the guilty.

God has given us this Gospel not merely for the purpose of securing to us life hereafter, but of making us sure of this life even now. It is a true and sure Gospel; so that he who believes it is made sure of being saved. If it could not make us sure, it would make us miserable; for to be told of such a salvation and such a glory, yet kept in doubt as to whether they are to be ours or not, must render us truly wretched. What a poor Gospel it must be, which leaves the man who believes it still in doubt as to whether he is a child of God, an unpardoned or a pardoned sinner! Till we have found forgiveness, we cannot be happy; we cannot serve God gladly or lovingly; but must be in sore bondage and gloom. This is the view of the matter which Scripture sets before us; telling us that salvation is a free, a sure, and a present gift. "He that believes is justified" (Acts 13:39). "He that believes has everlasting life" (John 3:36). The Bible gives no quarter to unbelief or doubting. It does not call it humility. It does not teach us to think better of ourselves for doubting. It does not countenance uncertainty or darkness.

THE REFORMATION: This was the view taken of the subject by our fathers, from the Reformation downwards. They held that a man ought to know that he is justified; and that it was Popery to teach uncertainty, or to set aside the full assurance of faith, or to hold that this sureness was not to be had from the beginning of a man's conversion, but only to be gathered up in process of years, by summing up his good feelings and good deeds, and concluding from his own excellences that he must be one of the elect, a man in favor with God. Our fathers believed that the jailor at Philippi rejoiced as soon as he received the good news which Paul preached to him (*Acts* 16:34). Our fathers believed that, "being justified by faith, we HAVE peace with God" (*Romans* 5:1), and that the life of a believing man is a life of known pardon; a life of peace with God; a life of which the outset was the settlement of the great question between himself and God; a life in which, as being a walk with God, the settlement of that question did not admit of being deferred or kept doubtful: for without felt agreement, without conscious reconciliation, intercourse was impossible. All the Reformation creeds and confessions take this for granted; assuming that the doctrine of uncertainty was one of the worst lies of Popery, the device and stronghold of a money-loving priesthood, who wished to keep people in suspense in order to make room for the dealings of priests and payments for pardon. If assurance be the right of every man who believes, then the priest's occupation is at an end; his craft is not only in danger, but gone. It was the want of assurance in his poor victims that enabled him to drive so prosperous a trade, and to coin money out of people's doubts. It was by this craft he had his wealth, and hence the hatred with which Rome and her priests have always hated the doctrine of assurance. It took the bread out of their mouths. If God pardons so freely, so simply, so surely, so immediately upon believing, alas for the priesthood! Who will pay them for absolution? Who will go to them to make sure that which God has already made sure in a more excellent way than theirs?

ROMAN CATHOLICISM: Romanists have always maintained that assurance is presumption; and it is remarkable that they quote, in defense of their opinion, the same passages which many modern Protestants do, such as, "Work out your salvation with fear and trembling;" the apostle's expression about being "a castaway;" "Let him that thinks he stands;" and the like. One of them, in reasoning with one of the English Reformers, speaks of "the presumptuous opinion of the certainty of grace and salvation, contrary to that which St. Paul counselleth, *Philippians* 2:12;" and the great Romish controversialists give the following reasons against assurance, which we abridge and translate:

I. No man certainly ought to disbelieve God's mercy and Christ's merits; but on account of his own imperfections, he ought to be fearful about his own grace, so that no one can certainly know that he has found favor with God.

II. It is not expedient that men should have certainty about their own grace; for certainty produces pride, while ignorance of this secret preserves and increases humility.

III. Assurance is the privilege of only a few favored ones, to whom God has revealed the singular benefit of the pardon of their sins.

IV. The most perfect men, when dying, have been humbled because of this uncertainty; and if some of the holiest men have been uncertain, is it credible that all believers ought to have assurance of their justification?

V. The best men may fall from faith; therefore there can be no assurance.

VI. The following passages confute the error of assurance:
1 Corinthians 10:12; *2 Corinthians* 6:1; *Romans* 11:20; *Philippians* 2:12

Such are the Popish arguments against assurance, and the conclusion to which the Council of Trent came was: "If any man shall say that justifying faith is confidence in the mercy of God, who remitteth sins for Christ's sake, or that it is by such confidence alone that we are justified, let him be accursed." Old John Foxe, who three hundred years ago wrote the history of the martyrs, remarks concerning the Pope's church, that it "left the poor consciences of men in perpetual doubt" (vol. 1, p. 78). This is a true saying. But it is true of many who earnestly protest against the Church of Rome. They not only teach doctrines which necessarily lead to doubting, and out of which no poor sinner could extract anything but uncertainty; but they inculcate doubting as a humble and excellent thing; a good preparation, nay, an indispensable qualification, for faith. The duty of doubting is in their theology much more obligatory than that of believing. The propriety and necessity of being uncertain they strongly insist upon; the blessedness of certainty they undervalue; the sinfulness of uncertainty they repudiate; the duty of being sure they deny. This same John Foxe, after showing that a man is saved not by working, but by believing, gives us the following specimen of "the horrible blindness and blasphemy" of the Church of Rome:

> *That faith wherewith a man firmly believeth and certainly assureth himself, that for Christ's sake his sins be forgiven him, and that he shall possess eternal life, is not faith, but rashness; not the persuasion of the Holy Ghost, but the presumption of human audacity.*

The above extract is from a Popish book of the time, and is a fair specimen of the Romish hatred of the doctrine of assurance. Its language is almost the same as that employed by many Protestants of our day. The Romanists held that a man is to believe in the mercy of God and the merits of Christ, but that this belief brought with it no assurance of justification; though possibly, if the man lived a very holy life, God might before he died reveal his grace to him, and give him assurance; which is precisely what many Protestants hold.

In opposition to this, our forefathers not only maintained that a man is justified by faith, but that he ought to know that he is justified, and that this knowledge of justification is the great root of a holy life. The Romanists did not quarrel with the word *assurance*; they did not hold it to be impossible: They held that men might get it, nay, that some very holy men had got it. But they affirmed that the only means of reaching the grace of assurance was by a holy life; that with the slow development of a holy life, assurance might develop itself, and that in the course of years, a man by numbering his good deeds, and ascertaining the amount of his holiness, might perhaps come to the conclusion that he was a child of God; but perhaps not. They were very strenuous in contending for this life of religious suspense, sad and dismal as it must be; because conscious justification, such as Luther contended for, shut out priesthood and penance; giving a man the joy of true liberty and divine fellowship at once, without the intervention of another party or the delay of an hour.

This conscious justification started the man upon a happy life, because relieved from the burden of doubt and the gloom of uncertainty; it made his religion bright and tranquil, because springing so sweetly from the certainty of his reconciliation to God; it delivered him from the cruel suspense and undefined fears which the want of assurance carries always with it; it rescued him from all temptations to self-righteousness, because not arising from any good thing in himself, it preserved him from pride and presumption, because it kept him from trying to magnify his own goodness in order to extract assurance out of it; it drew him away from self to Christ, from what he was doing to what Christ had done; thus making Christ, not self, the basis and the center of his new being; it made him more and more dissatisfied with self, and all that self-contained, but more and more satisfied with Jesus and his fulness; it taught him to rest his confidence toward God, not on his satisfaction with self, not on the development of his own holiness, not on the amount of his graces and prayers and doings, but simply on the complete work of him in whom God is well pleased.

The Romanists acquiesced in the general formula of the Protestants, that salvation was all of Christ, and that we are to believe on him in order to get it. But they resisted the idea that a man, on believing, knows that he is saved. They might even have admitted the terms "justification by faith," provided it was conceded that this justification was to be known only to God, hidden from the sinner who believes. They did not much heed the mere form of words, and some of them went apparently a long way to the Protestant doctrine. But that which was essential to their system was, that in whatever way justification took place, it should be kept secret from the sinner himself, so that he should remain without assurance for years, perhaps all his life. Unconscious justification by faith suited their system of darkness quite as well as justification by works. For it was not merely the kind of justification that they hated, but the sinner's knowing it, and having peace with God simply in believing, without waiting for years of doing. No doubt they objected to free justification in the Protestant sense; but the force of their objection lies not so much against its being free, as against the sinner being sure of it. For they saw well enough that if they could only introduce uncertainty at any part of the process, their end was gained. For to remove such uncertainty the Church must be called in; and this was all they wanted.

The doctrine, then, that makes uncertainty necessary, and that affirms that this uncertainty can only be removed by the development of a holy life, is the old Popish one, though uttered by Protestants. Luther condemned it; Bellarmine maintained it. And many of the modern objections to assurance, on the part of some Protestants, are a mere reproduction of old Romish arguments, urged again and again, against justification by faith. There is hardly one objection made to a man's being sure of his justification which would not apply, and which have not been applied, against his being justified by faith at all. If the common arguments against assurance turn out valid, they cannot stop short of establishing justification by works. Salvation by believing, and assurance only by means of working, are not very compatible.

The interval, which is thus created between God's act of justifying us, and his letting us know that he has justified us, is a singular one, of which Scripture certainly takes no cognizance. This interval of suspense (be it longer or shorter) which Romanists have created for the purpose of giving full scope to priestly interposition, and which some Protestants keep up in order to save us from pride and presumption, is not acknowledged in the Bible any more than purgatory. An intermediate state in the life to come, during which the soul is neither pardoned nor unpardoned, neither in Heaven nor Hell, is thought needful by Romanists for purging out sin and developing holiness; but then this interval of gloom is one of man's creation. An intermediate state in this life, during which a sinner, though believing in Jesus, is not to know whether he is justified or not, is reckoned equally needful by some Protestants, as a necessary means of producing holiness, and through holiness leading perhaps ere life close to assurance; but then of this sorrowful interval, this present purgatory, which would make a Christian's life so dreary and fearful, the Scripture says nothing. It is a human delusion borrowed from Popery, and based upon the dislike of the human heart to have immediate peace, immediate adoption, and immediate fellowship. The self-righteous heart of man craves an interval of the above kind as a space for the exercise of his religiousness, while free from the responsibility for a holy and unworldly life which conscious justification imposes on the conscience.

But it will be greatly worth our while to see what Romanists have said upon this subject; for their errors help us much in understanding the truth. It will be seen that it was against present peace with God that Rome contended; and that it was in defense of this present peace, this immediate certainty, that the Reformers did battle so strenuously, as a matter of life and death. The great Popish Assembly, the "Council of Trent" in 1547, took up these points concerning faith and grace. Nor was that body content with condemning assurance; they proclaimed it an accursed thing, and pronounced an anathema against everyone who affirmed that justifying faith is "confidence in the mercy of God." They denounced the man as a heretic who should hold "the confidence and certainty of the remission of his sins." Yet they had a theory of a justification by faith. We give it in their own words, as it corresponds strikingly with the process which is prescribed by some Protestants as the means of arriving, after long years, at the knowledge of our justification:

> *The beginning of justification proceedeth from preventing grace. The manner of the preparation is, first to believe the divine revelations and promises, and knowing oneself to be a sinner, to turn from the fear of God's justice to his mercy, to hope for pardon from him, and therefore to begin to love him and hate sin, to begin a new life, and keep the commandments of God. Justification follows this preparation.*

This theory of a gradual justification, or a gradual approach to justification, is that held by many Protestants, and made use of by them for resisting the truth of immediate forgiveness of sin and peace with God. Then comes another sentence of the Council, which expresses truly the modem theory of non-assurance, and the common excuse for doubting, when men say, "We are not doubting Christ, we are only doubting ourselves." The Romish divines assert:

> *No one ought to doubt the mercy of God, the merits of Christ, and the efficacy of the sacraments; but in regard to his own indisposition he may doubt, because he cannot know by certainly of infallible faith, that he has obtained grace.*

Here sinners are taught to believe in God's mercy and in Christ's merits, yet still to go on doubting as to the results of that belief, namely, sure peace with God. Truly self-righteousness, whether resting on works or on feelings, whether in Popery or Protestantism, is the same thing, and the root of the same errors, and the source of the same determination not to allow immediate certainty to the sinner from the belief of the good news. This Popish council took special care that the doctrine of assurance should be served with their most pointed curses. All the "errors of Martin Luther" were by them traced back to this twofold root, that a man is justified by faith, and that he ought to know that he is justified. They thus accuse the German Reformer of inventing his doctrine of immediate and conscious justification for the purpose of destroying the sinner's works of repentance, which by their necessary imperfection make room for indulgences. They call this free justification, a thing unheard of before – a thing which not only makes good works unnecessary, but sets a man free from any obligation to obey the law of God.

It would appear that the learned doctors of the Council were bewildered with the Lutheran doctrine. The schoolmen had never discussed it, nor even stated it. It had no place either among the beliefs or misbeliefs of the past. It had not been maintained as a truth, nor impugned as a heresy, so far as they knew. It was an absolute novelty. They did not comprehend it, and of course misrepresented it. As to original sin, that had been so often discussed by the schoolmen, that all Romish divines and priests were familiar with it in one aspect or another. On it, therefore, the Council were at home, and could frame their curses easily, and with some point. But the Lutheran doctrine of justification brought them to a stand. Thus the old translator of Paul Sarpi's *History* puts it:

> The opinion of Luther concerning justifying faith, that it is a confidence and certain persuasion of the promise of God, with the consequences that follow, of the distinction between the law and the gospel, etc., had never been thought of by any school writers, and therefore never confuted or discussed, so that the divines had work enough to understand the meaning of the Lutheran propositions.

Luther's doctrine of the will's bondage they were indignant at, as making man a stone or a machine. His doctrine of righteousness by faith horrified them, as the inlet of all laxity and wickedness. Protestant doctrines were to them absurdities no less than heresies. Nor was it merely the Church, the Fathers, and tradition that they stood upon. The schools and the schoolmen! This was their watchword; for hitherto these scholastic doctors had been, at least for centuries, the body-guard of the church. Under their learning and subtleties and casuistries, priests and bishops had always taken refuge. Indeed, without them, the Roman Church was helpless, as far as logic was concerned. When she had to argue, she must call in these metaphysical divines; though generally by force and terror she contrived to supersede all necessity for reasoning. Three men in the Council showed some independence: a Dominican friar, by name Ambrosius Catarinus; a Spanish Franciscan, by name Andreas de Vega; and a Carmelite, by name Antoninus Marinarus. The "Heremites" of the order to which Luther originally belonged were especially blind and bitter, their leader Seripandus outdoing all in zeal against Luther and his heresy.

The jewel of assurance is best kept in the cabinet of the heart.
- *Thomas Watson*

If the priesthood of all believers is the first fruit of justification,
"assurance" is the second. - *John R.W. Stott*

Assurance of better things makes the soul sing care away, as that martyr
said, "My soul is turned to her rest; I have taken a sweet nap in Christ's
lap, and therefore I will now sing care away, and will be careless
according to my name." - *Thomas Brooks*

Sanctification is the seed; assurance is the flower which grows out of it.
- *Thomas Watson*

The inward witness, son, the inward witness; that is proof, the strongest
proof of Christianity. - *Samuel Wesley*

DAY 30

ASSURANCE OF SALVATION
BY HORATIUS BONAR
PART 2

PAUL AND LUTHER,

Compelled, in the investigation of the subject, to pass beyond Luther to Luther's Master, they were sorely puzzled. To overlook him was impossible, for the Protestants appealed to him; to condemn him would not have been wise. They were obliged to admit the bitter truth that Paul had said that a man is justified by faith. They had maintained the strict literality of "This is my body;" must they admit the equal literality of "justified by faith"? Or may this latter expression not be qualified and overlaid by scholastic ingenuity, or set aside by an authoritative denial in the name of the Church? At the Council of Trent both these methods were tried. It was not Luther only who laid such stress upon the doctrine of free justification. His adversaries were wise enough to do the same. They saw in it the root or foundation-stone of the whole Reformation. If it falls, Popery stands erect, and may do what she pleases with the consciences of men. If it stands, Popery is overthrown; her hold on men's consciences is gone; her priestly power is at an end, and men have directly to do with the Lord Jesus Christ in Heaven, and not with any pretended vicar upon Earth, or any of his priests or seven sacraments. "All the errors of Martin are resolved into that point," said the bishops of the Council; and they added, "He that will establish the [Roman] Catholic doctrine must overthrow the heresy of righteousness by faith only."

But did not Paul say the same thing as Luther has said? Did he not say, "To him that works not, but believes on him that justifies the ungodly, his faith is counted for righteousness"? (*Romans* 4:20). Yes; but we may use some liberties with Paul's words, which we cannot do with Luther's. It would not do to refute Paul; but it is quite safe to demonstrate that Luther is wrong, and is at variance with the [Roman] Church. Let us then assail Luther, and leave Paul alone. Now Luther has said such things as the following:

I.   Faith without works is sufficient for salvation, and alone justifies.

II. Justifying faith is a sure trust, by which one believes that his sins are remitted for Christ's sake; and they that are justified are to believe certainly that their sins are remitted.

III. By faith only we are able to appear before God, who neither regards nor has need of our works; faith only purifying us.

IV. No previous disposition is necessary to justification; neither does faith justify because it disposes us, but because it is a means or instrument by which the promise and grace of God are laid hold on and received.

V. All the works of men, even the most sanctified, are sin.

VI. Though the just ought to believe that his works are sins, yet he ought to be assured that they are not imputed.

These were some of Luther's propositions which required to be confuted. That they looked wonderfully like the doctrines of the Apostle Paul only made the confutation more necessary.

That "faith justifies," the bishops said, we must admit, because the apostle has said so; but as to what faith is, and how it justifies, is hard to say. Faith has many meanings (some said nine, others fifteen; some modern Protestants have said the same); and then, even admitting that faith justifies, it cannot do so without good dispositions, without penance, without religious performances, without sacraments. By introducing all these ingredients into faith, they easily turned it into a work; or by placing them on the same level with faith, they nullified (without positively denying) justification by faith. Ingenious men! Thus to overthrow the truth, while professing to admit and explain it!

In this ingenious perversity, they have had many successors, and that in churches which rejected Rome and its Council. "Christ crucified" is the burden of the message which God has sent to man. "Christ died for our sins, according to the Scriptures." The reception of this Gospel is eternal life; and non-reception or rejection of it is everlasting death. "This is the record, that God has given to us eternal life, and this life is in his Son." The belief of the Gospel saves; the belief of the promise annexed to that Gospel makes us sure of this salvation personally. It is not the belief of our belief that assures us of pardon, and gives us a good conscience towards God; but our belief of what God has promised to everyone who believes his Gospel – that is eternal life. **"Believe in the Lord Jesus Christ, and you shall be saved."**

What is God to me? That is the first question that rises up to an inquiring soul. And the second is like unto it – What am I to God? On these two questions hangs all religion, as well as all joy and life to the immortal spirit. If God is for me, and I am for God, all is well. If God is not for me, and if I am not for God, all is ill (*Romans* 8:31). If he takes my side, and if I take his, there is nothing to fear, either in this world or in that which is to come. If he is not on my side, and if I am not on his, then what can I do but fear? Terror in such a case must be as natural and inevitable as in a burning house or a sinking vessel. Or, if I do not know whether God is for me or not, I can have no rest. In a matter such as this, my soul seeks certainty, not uncertainty. I must know that God is for me, else I must remain in the sadness of unrest and terror. Insofar as my actual safety is concerned, everything depends on God being for me; and insofar as my present peace is concerned, everything depends on my knowing that God is for me. Nothing can calm the tempest of my soul, save the knowledge that I am his, and that he is mine.

Thus the questions about assurance resolve themselves into that of the knowledge of our relationship to God. To an Arminian, who denies election and the perseverance of the saints, the knowledge of our present reconciliation to God might bring with it no assurance of final salvation; for, according to him, we may be in reconciliation today, and out of it tomorrow; but to a Calvinist there can be no such separation. He who is once reconciled is reconciled forever; and the knowledge of filial relationship just now is the assurance of eternal salvation. Indeed, apart from God's electing love, there can be no such thing as assurance. It becomes an impossibility. Assurance does not save us; and they have erred who have spoken of assurance as indispensable to salvation. For we are not saved by believing in our own salvation, nor by believing anything whatsoever about ourselves. We are saved by what we believe about the Son of God and his righteousness. The Gospel believed saves; not the believing in our own faith.

The being in a state of grace will yield a man a heaven hereafter, but the seeing of himself in this estate will yield him both a heaven here and a heaven hereafter; it will render him doubly blest, blest in heaven. and blest in his own conscience. - *Thomas Brooks*

The assured Christian is more motion than notion, more work than word, more life than lip, more hand than tongue. - *Thomas Brooks*

He "binds up the broken-hearted" (Isa. 61:1). As a mother is tenderest toward the most diseased and weakest child, so does Christ most mercifully incline to the weakest. Likewise he puts an instinct into the weakest things to rely upon something stronger than themselves for support. The vine steadies itself upon the elm, and the weakest creatures often have the strongest shelters. The consciousness of the church's weakness makes her willing to lean on her Beloved and to hide herself under his wing. - *Richard Sibbes*

Assurance makes most for your comfort but holiness makes most for God's honour. - *Thomas Brooks*

Faith cannot be lost, but assurance may; therefore assurance is not faith. - *Thomas Brooks*

DAY 31

THE GOLDEN KEY TO OPEN HIDDEN TREASURES
BY THOMAS BROOKS

May you have power to grasp how wide and long and high and deep is the love of Christ, and to know this love that surpasses knowledge. - Ephesians 3:18-19

OH, SUCH WAS CHRIST'S transcendent love that man's extreme misery could not abate it. The deploredness of man's condition did but heighten the holy flame of Christ's love. It is as high as heaven, who can reach it? It is as low as hell, who can understand it?

Heaven, with all its glory, could not contain Him. Neither could all hell's torments make Him refrain! Such was His perfect matchless love to fallen and miserable man. That Christ's love should extend to the ungodly, to sinners, to enemies who were in rebellion against Him; yes, not only to but that He should hug them in His arms, lodge them in His bosom, is the highest degree of love!

IT IS ASTONISHING...

- ♦ That Christ should come from the eternal bosom of His Father to a region of sorrow and death
- ♦ That God should be manifested in the flesh
- ♦ That the Creator should made a creature
- ♦ That He who was clothed with glory should be wrapped with rags of flesh
- ♦ That He who filled heaven should be cradled in a feeding trough
- ♦ That the God of strength should be weary
- ♦ That the judge of all men should be condemned
- ♦ That the God of life should be put to death
- ♦ That He would do all this for man, for fallen man, for miserable man, for worthless man is beyond all conception

The sharp sufferings of our Lord Jesus Christ, from the cradle to the cross, does above all other things, speak out the transcendent love of Jesus Christ to poor sinners. That wrath, that *great* wrath, that *fierce* wrath, that *pure* wrath, that *infinite* wrath, that *matchless* wrath of an angry God, which was so terribly impressed upon the soul of Christ, all this wrath He patiently underwent, that sinners might be saved, and that "He might bring many sons unto glory."

Oh wonder at the greatness of His love, which made our dear Lord Jesus lay down His life, to save us from hell, and to bring us to heaven! Oh unspeakable love! It was the golden link of love, which alone fastened Christ to the cross, and made Him die freely for us!

Christ's love is beyond all measure, for...

♦ **Time** did not begin it, and time shall never end it
♦ **Place** does not bound it
♦ **Sin** does not exceed it
♦ **Tongues** cannot express it
♦ **Minds** cannot conceive it.

Well may we spend all our days in admiring and adoring of Christ's wonderful love, and be always ravished with the thoughts of it.

May you experience the love of Christ, though it is so great you will never fully understand it. - Ephesians 3:19

A soul under assurance is unwilling to go to heaven without company.
- *Thomas Brooks*

Perfect signs of grace can never spring from imperfect grace.
- *Thomas Brooks*

Without the diligent use of means a lazy Christian has no right to expect to receive assurance. - *Thomas Brooks*

Feelings of confidence about our salvation need to be tested before they are trusted. - *J.I. Packer*

There is more mercy in Christ than sin in us. - *Richard Sibbes*

A DEBTOR TO MERCY ALONE

Augustus Montague Toplady

A debtor to mercy alone,
Of covenant mercy I sing;
Nor fear, with Thy righteousness on,
My person and offering to bring.
The terrors of law and of God
With me can have nothing to do;
My Savior's obedience and blood
Hide all my transgressions from view.

The work which His goodness began,
The arm of His strength will complete;
His promise is yea and amen,
And never was forfeited yet.
Things future, nor things that are now,
Not all things below nor above
Can make Him His purpose forego,
Or sever my soul from His love.

My name from the palms of His hands
Eternity will not erase;
Impressed on His heart it remains
In marks of indelible grace.
Yes, I to the end shall endure,
As sure as the earnest is given
More happy, but not more secure,
The glorified spirits in heaven.

JESUS, THY BLOOD AND RIGHTEOUSNESS

Nikolaus Ludwig von Zinzendorf

Jesus, Thy blood and righteousness
My beauty are, my glorious dress;
'Midst flaming worlds, in these arrayed,
With joy shall I lift up my head.

Bold shall I stand in Thy great day;

For who aught to my charge shall lay?
Fully absolved through these I am
From sin and fear, from guilt and shame.

The holy, meek, unspotted Lamb,
Who from the Father's bosom came,
Who died for me, e'en me to atone,
Now for my Lord and God I own.

Lord, I believe Thy precious blood,
Which, at the mercy seat of God,
Forever doth for sinners plead,
For me, e'en for my soul, was shed.

Lord, I believe were sinners more
Than sands upon the ocean shore,
Thou hast for all a ransom paid,
For all a full atonement made.

When from the dust of death I rise
To claim my mansion in the skies,
Ev'n then this shall be all my plea,
Jesus hath lived, hath died, for me.

This spotless robe the same appears,
When ruined nature sinks in years;
No age can change its glorious hue,
The robe of Christ is ever new.

Jesus, the endless praise to Thee,
Whose boundless mercy hath for me—
For me a full atonement made,
An everlasting ransom paid.

O let the dead now hear Thy voice;
Now bid Thy banished ones rejoice;
Their beauty this, their glorious dress,
Jesus, Thy blood and righteousness.

NOT WHAT MY HANDS HAVE DONE
Horatius Bonar

Not what my hands have done can save my guilty soul;

Not what my toiling flesh has borne can make my spirit whole.
Not what I feel or do can give me peace with God;
Not all my prayers and sighs and tears can bear my awful load.

Your voice alone, O Lord, can speak to me of grace;
Your power alone, O Son of God, can all my sin erase.
No other work but Yours, no other blood will do;
No strength but that which is divine can bear me safely through.

Thy work alone, O Christ, can ease this weight of sin;
Thy blood alone, O Lamb of God, can give me peace within.
Thy love to me, O God, not mine, O Lord, to Thee,
Can rid me of this dark unrest, And set my spirit free.

I bless the Christ of God; I rest on love divine;
And with unfaltering lip and heart I call this Savior mine.
His cross dispels each doubt; I bury in His tomb
Each thought of unbelief and fear, each lingering shade of gloom.

I praise the God of grace; I trust His truth and might;
He calls me His, I call Him mine, My God, my joy and light.
'Tis He Who saveth me, and freely pardon gives;
I love because He loveth me, I live because He lives.

THE CHURCH'S ONE FOUNDATION

Samuel John Stone

The Church's one foundation
is Jesus Christ her Lord;
she is his new creation,
by water and the word:
from heaven he came and sought her
to be his holy bride;
with his own blood he bought her,
and for her life he died.

Elect from every nation,
yet one o'er all the earth,
her charter of salvation,
one Lord, one faith, one birth;
one holy Name she blesses,
partakes one holy food,
and to one hope she presses,

with every grace endued.

The Church shall never perish!
Her dear Lord to defend,
To guide, sustain, and cherish,
Is with her to the end:
Though there be those who hate her,
And false sons in her pale,
Against both foe or traitor
She ever shall prevail.

Though with a scornful wonder
men see her sore oppressed,
by schisms rent asunder,
by heresies distressed;
yet saints their watch are keeping,
their cry goes up, "How long?"
and soon the night of weeping
shall be the morn of song.

Mid toil and tribulation,
and tumult of her war
she waits the consummation
of peace for evermore;
till with the vision glorious
her longing eyes are blessed,
and the great Church victorious
shall be the Church at rest.

Yet she on earth hath union
with God, the Three in one,
and mystic sweet communion
with those whose rest is won.
O happy ones and holy!
Lord, give us grace that we

like them, the meek and lowly,
on high may dwell with thee.

CROWN HIM WITH MANY CROWNS
George Job Elvey

Crown Him with many crowns, the Lamb upon His throne.
Hark! How the heavenly anthem drowns all music but its own.

Awake, my soul, and sing of Him who died for thee,
And hail Him as thy matchless King through all eternity.

Crown Him the virgin's Son, the God incarnate born,
Whose arm those crimson trophies won which now His brow adorn;
Fruit of the mystic rose, as of that rose the stem;
The root whence mercy ever flows, the Babe of Bethlehem.

Crown Him the Son of God, before the worlds began,
And ye who tread where He hath trod, crown Him the Son of Man;
Who every grief hath known that wrings the human breast,
And takes and bears them for His own, that all in Him may rest.

Crown Him the Lord of life, who triumphed over the grave,
And rose victorious in the strife for those He came to save.
His glories now we sing, who died, and rose on high,
Who died eternal life to bring, and lives that death may die.

Crown Him the Lord of peace, whose power a scepter sways
From pole to pole, that wars may cease, and all be prayer and praise.
His reign shall know no end, and round His pierced feet
Fair flowers of paradise extend their fragrance ever sweet.

Crown Him the Lord of love, behold His hands and side,
Those wounds, yet visible above, in beauty glorified.
No angel in the sky can fully bear that sight,
But downward bends his burning eye at mysteries so bright.

Crown Him the Lord of Heaven, enthroned in worlds above,
Crown Him the King to Whom is given the wondrous name of Love.
Crown Him with many crowns, as thrones before Him fall;
Crown Him, ye kings, with many crowns, for He is King of all.

Crown Him the Lord of lords, who over all doth reign,
Who once on earth, the incarnate Word, for ransomed sinners slain,
Now lives in realms of light, where saints with angels sing
Their songs before Him day and night, their God, Redeemer, King.

Crown Him the Lord of years, the Potentate of time,
Creator of the rolling spheres, ineffably sublime.
All hail, Redeemer, hail! For Thou has died for me;
Thy praise and glory shall not fail throughout eternity.

A MIGHTY FORTRESS IS OUR GOD

Martin Luther

A mighty fortress is our God,
a bulwark never failing;
our helper he, amid the flood
of mortal ills prevailing.
For still our ancient foe
does seek to work us woe;
his craft and power are great,
and armed with cruel hate,
on earth is not his equal.

Did we in our own strength confide,
our striving would be losing,
were not the right Man on our side,
the Man of God's own choosing.
You ask who that may be?
Christ Jesus, it is he;
Lord Sabaoth his name,
from age to age the same;
and he must win the battle.

And though this world, with devils filled,
should threaten to undo us,
we will not fear, for God has willed
his truth to triumph through us.
The prince of darkness grim,
we tremble not for him;
his rage we can endure,

for lo! his doom is sure;
one little word shall fell him.

That Word above all earthly powers
no thanks to them abideth;
the Spirit and the gifts are ours
through him who with us sideth.
Let goods and kindred go,
this mortal life also;
the body they may kill:
God's truth abideth still;
his kingdom is forever!

HOW FIRM A FOUNDATION

John Rippon

How firm a foundation, ye saints of the Lord,
Is laid for your faith in His excellent word!
What more can He say than to you He hath said,
To you who for refuge to Jesus have fled?

Fear not, I am with thee, O be not dismayed,
For I am thy God, and will still give thee aid;
I'll strengthen thee, help thee, and cause thee to stand,
Upheld by My righteous, omnipotent hand.

When through the deep waters I call thee to go,
The rivers of sorrow shall not overflow;
For I will be with thee, thy troubles to bless,
And sanctify to thee thy deepest distress.

When through fiery trials thy pathway shall lie,
My grace, all sufficient, shall be thy supply;
The flame shall not hurt thee; I only design
Thy dross to consume, and thy gold to refine.

E'en down to old age all My people shall prove
My sovereign, eternal, unchangeable love;
And then, when grey hairs shall their temples adorn,
Like lambs they shall still in My bosom be borne.

The soul that on Jesus hath leaned for repose,
I will not, I will not desert to his foes;
That soul, though all hell should endeavor to shake,
I'll never, no, never, no, never forsake!

COME THOU FOUNT
Robert Robinson

Come, Thou Fount of every blessing
Tune my heart to sing Thy grace
Streams of mercy never ceasing
Call for songs of loudest praise
Teach me some melodious sonnet
Sung by flaming tongues above
Praise the name! I'm fixed upon it
Name of Thy redeeming love

Hitherto Thy love has blessed me
Thou hast brought me to this place
And I know Thy hand will bring me
Safely home by Thy good grace
Jesus sought me when a stranger
Wandering from the fold of God
He, to rescue me from danger
Interposed His precious blood

Oh to grace how great a debtor
Daily I'm constrained to be
Let Thy goodness, like a fetter
Bind my wandering heart to Thee
Prone to wander, Lord, I feel it
Prone to leave the God I love
Here's my heart, oh take and seal it
Seal it for Thy courts above

Oh that day when freed from sinning
I shall see Thy lovely face
Full arrayed in blood-washed linen

How I'll sing Thy sovereign grace
Come, my Lord, no longer tarry
Bring Thy promises to pass
For I know Thy pow'r will keep me
Till I'm home with Thee at last

THERE IS A FOUNTAIN
William Cowper

There is a fountain filled with blood
Drawn from Immanuel's veins;
And sinners, plunged beneath that flood,

Lose all their guilty stains:
Lose all their guilty stains,
Lose all their guilty stains;
And sinners, plunged beneath that flood,
Lose all their guilty stains.

The dying thief rejoiced to see
That fountain in his day;
And there may I, though vile as he,
Wash all my sins away:
Wash all my sins away,
Wash all my sins away;
And there may I, though vile as he,
Wash all my sins away.

Dear dying Lamb, Thy precious blood
Shall never lose its power,
Till all the ransomed ones of God
Be saved, to sin no more:
Be saved, to sin no more,
Be saved, to sin no more;
Till all the ransomed ones of God,
Be saved to sin no more.

E'er since by faith I saw the stream
Thy flowing wounds supply,
Redeeming love has been my theme,
And shall be till I die:
And shall be till I die,

And shall be till I die;
Redeeming love has been my theme,
And shall be till I die.

When this poor lisping, stammering tongue
Lies silent in the grave,
Then in a nobler, sweeter song,

I'll sing Thy power to save:
I'll sing Thy power to save,
I'll sing Thy power to save;
Then in a nobler, sweeter song,
I'll sing Thy power to save.

PRAISE TO THE LORD, THE ALMIGHTY

Joachim Neander

Praise to the Lord, the Almighty, the King of creation!
O my soul, praise Him, for He is thy health and salvation!
All ye who hear, now to His temple draw near;
Praise Him in glad adoration.

Praise to the Lord, who o'er all things so wondrously reigneth,
Shelters thee under His wings, yea, so gently sustaineth!
Hast thou not seen how thy desires e'er have been
Granted in what He ordaineth?

Praise to the Lord, who doth prosper thy work and defend thee;
Surely His goodness and mercy here daily attend thee;
Ponder anew what the Almighty can do,
If with His love He befriend thee.

Praise to the Lord, who, when tempests their warfare are waging,
Who, when the elements madly around thee are raging,
Biddeth them cease, turneth their fury to peace,
Whirlwinds and waters assuaging.

Praise to the Lord, who, when darkness of sin is abounding,
Who, when the godless do triumph, all virtue confounding,
Sheddeth His light, chaseth the horrors of night,
Saints with His mercy surrounding.

Praise to the Lord, oh, let all that is in me adore Him!
All that hath life and breath, come now with praises before Him;
Let the Amen sound from His people again,
Gladly for aye we adore Him.

IT IS WELL
Horatio Spafford

When peace, like a river, attendeth my way,
When sorrows like sea billows roll;
Whatever my lot, Thou hast taught me to say,
It is well, it is well with my soul.

It is well with my soul,
It is well, it is well with my soul.

Though Satan should buffet, though trials should come,
Let this blest assurance control,
That Christ hath regarded my helpless estate,
And hath shed His own blood for my soul.

My sin - oh, the bliss of this glorious thought!
My sin, not in part but the whole,

Is nailed to the cross, and I bear it no more,
Praise the Lord, praise the Lord, O my soul!

For me, be it Christ, be it Christ hence to live:
If Jordan above me shall roll,
No pang shall be mine, for in death as in life
Thou wilt whisper Thy peace to my soul.

But, Lord, 'tis for Thee, for Thy coming we wait,
The sky, not the grave, is our goal;
Oh, trump of the angel! Oh, voice of the Lord!
Blessed hope, blessed rest of my soul!

And Lord, haste the day when the faith shall be sight,
The clouds be rolled back as a scroll;
The trump shall resound, and the Lord shall descend,
Even so, it is well with my soul.

THE SOLID ROCK
Edward Mote

My hope is built on nothing less
Than Jesus' blood and righteousness;
I dare not trust the sweetest frame,
But wholly lean on Jesus' name.

On Christ, the solid Rock, I stand;
All other ground is sinking sand,
All other ground is sinking sand.

When darkness veils His lovely face,
I rest on His unchanging grace;
In every high and stormy gale,
My anchor holds within the veil.

His oath, His covenant, His blood
Support me in the whelming flood;
When all around my soul gives way,
He then is all my hope and stay.

When He shall come with trumpet sound,
Oh, may I then in Him be found;
Dressed in His righteousness alone,
Faultless to stand before the throne.

ROCK OF AGES
Augustus Toplady

Rock of Ages, cleft for me,
Let me hide myself in Thee;
Let the water and the blood,
From Thy wounded side which flowed,
Be of sin the double cure,
Save from wrath and make me pure.

Not the labor of my hands
Can fulfill Thy law's demands;
Could my zeal no respite know,
Could my tears forever flow,
All for sin could not atone;
Thou must save, and Thou alone.

Nothing in my hand I bring,
Simply to Thy cross I cling;
Naked, come to Thee for dress;

Helpless, look to Thee for grace;

Foul, I to the fountain fly;
Wash me, Savior, or I die.

While I draw this fleeting breath,
When my eyes shall close in death,
When I rise to worlds unknown,
And behold Thee on Thy throne,
Rock of Ages, cleft for me,
Let me hide myself in Thee.

WHEN I SURVEY THE WONDROUS CROSS
Isaac Watts

When we survey the wondrous cross
On which the Lord of glory died,
Our richest gain we count but loss,
And pour contempt on all our pride.

Our God forbid that we should boast,
Save in the death of Christ, our Lord;
All the vain things that charm us most,
We'd sacrifice them to His blood.

There from His head, His hands, His feet,
Sorrow and love flowed mingled down;
Did e'er such love and sorrow meet,
Or thorns compose so rich a crown?

His dying crimson, from His head
Spreads o'er His body on the tree;
To all the world then am I dead,
And all the world is dead to me.

Were the whole realm of nature ours,
That were an offering far too small;
Love that transcends our highest pow'rs,
Demands our heart, our life, our all.

BE THOU MY VISION
Dallan Forgaill

Be Thou my vision, O Lord of my heart;
Naught be all else to me, save that Thou art;
Thou my best thought, by day or by night;
Waking or sleeping, Thy presence my light.

Be Thou my wisdom, and Thou my true Word;
I ever with Thee and Thou with me, Lord;
Thou my great Father and I, Thy true son;
Thou in me dwelling, and I with Thee one.

Be Thou my battle Shield, Sword for the fight;
Be Thou my Dignity, Thou my Delight;
Thou my soul's Shelter, Thou my high Tow'r:
Raise Thou me heav'nward, O Pow'r of my pow'r.

Riches I heed not, nor man's empty praise;
Thou mine inheritance, now and always;
Thou and Thou only, first in my heart;
O King of glory, my treasure Thou art.

O King of glory, my victory won;
Rule and reign in me 'til Thy will be done;
Heart of my own heart, whatever befall;
Still be my vision, O Ruler of all.

REJOICE, THE LORD IS KING!
Charles Wesley

Rejoice, the Lord is King!
Your Lord and King adore!
Rejoice, give thanks, and
sing and triumph evermore:
Lift up your heart,
lift up your voice!
Rejoice, again
I say, rejoice!

Jesus, the Savior, reigns,
The God of truth and love;
When He had purged our stains,
He took His seat above:
Lift up your heart,
lift up your voice!
Rejoice, again
I say, rejoice!

He sits at God's right hand
Til all His foes submit,
And bow to his command
and fall beneath His feet.
Lift up your heart,

lift up your voice!
Rejoice, again
I say, rejoice!

He all our foes shall quell,
shall all our sins destroy,
and every bosom swell
with pure seraphic joy!
Lift up your heart,
lift up your voice!
Rejoice, again
I say, rejoice!

His kingdom cannot fail,
He rules o'er earth and heaven;
The keys of death and grave
Are to our Jesus given:
Lift up your heart,
lift up your voice!
Rejoice, again
I say, rejoice!

Rejoice in glorious hope!
Our Lord the judge shall come,
And take His servants up
To their eternal home:
(And the last two lines of this verse were originally)
We soon shall hear
the archangel's voice,
the trump of God
shall sound, rejoice!

O LOVE, HOW DEEP

Thomas á Kempis

O love, how deep, how broad, how high,
it fills the heart with ecstasy,
that God, the Son of God, should take
our mortal form for mortals' sake!

He sent no angel to our race
Of higher or of lower place,
But bore the robe of human frame
Himself, and to this lost world came.

For us baptized, for us he bore
his holy fast and hungered sore,
for us temptation sharp he knew;
for us the tempter overthrew.

For us he prayed; for us he taught;
for us his daily works he wrought;
by words and signs and actions thus
still seeking not himself, but us.

For us to evil power betrayed,
scourged, mocked, in purple robe arrayed,
for us he bore the cross and death,
for us at length gave up his breath.

For us he died and rose again;
for us he went on high to reign;
for us he sent his Spirit here,
to guide, to strengthen, and to cheer.

To Him whose boundless love has won
Salvation for us through His Son;
To God the Father, glory be
Both now and through eternity.

WE COME, O CHRIST, TO THEE
Edith Margaret Clarkson

We come, O Christ to thee,
true Son of God and man,
by whom all things consist,
in whom all life began:
in thee alone we live and move,
and have our being in thy love.

Thou art the Way to God,
thy blood our ransom paid;
in thee we face our Judge
and Maker unafraid.
Before the throne absolved we stand,
thy love has met thy law's demand.

Thou art the living Truth!
All wisdom dwells in thee,
thou source of every skill,
eternal Verity!
Thou great I AM! In thee we rest,
sure answer to our every quest.

Thou only art true Life,
to know thee is to live
the more abundant life
that earth can never give:
O risen Lord! We live in thee:
and thou in us eternally!

We worship thee, Lord Christ,
our Savior and our King,
to thee our youth and strength
adoringly we bring:
so fill our hearts that men may see
thy life in us, and turn to thee!

STRICKEN SMITTEN AND AFFLICTED
Thomas Kelly

Stricken, smitten, and afflicted,
see him dying on the tree!
'Tis the Christ, by man rejected;
yes, my soul, 'tis he, 'tis he.
'Tis the long-expected Prophet,
David's Son, yet David's Lord;
proofs I see sufficient of it:
'tis the true and faithful Word.

Tell me, as you hear him groaning,
was there ever grief like his,
friends through fear his cause disowning,
foes insulting his distress?
Many hands were raised to wound him,
none would intervene to save;
but the deepest stroke that pierced him
was the stroke that justice gave.

If you think of sin but lightly
nor suppose the evil great,
here you see its nature rightly,
here its guilt may estimate.
Mark the sacrifice appointed,
see who bears the awful load;
'tis the Word, the Lord's anointed,
Son of Man and Son of God.

Here we have a firm foundation,
here the refuge of the lost:
Christ, the Rock of our salvation,
is the name of which we boast;
Lamb of God, for sinners wounded,
sacrifice to cancel guilt!
None shall ever be confounded
who on him their hope have built.

BE STILL MY SOUL
Kathrina von Schlegel

Be still, my soul; the Lord is on your side;
bear patiently the cross of grief or pain;
leave to your God to order and provide;
in ev'ry change he faithful will remain.

Be still, my soul; your best, your heav'nly friend
through thorny ways leads to a joyful end.

Be still, my soul; your God will undertake
to guide the future as he has the past;
your hope, your confidence, let nothing shake;
all now mysterious shall be bright at last.
Be still, my soul; the waves and winds still know
his voice who ruled them while he lived below.

Be still, my soul; when dearest friends depart
and all is darkened in the vale of tears,
then you will better know his love, his heart,
who comes to soothe your sorrows and your fears.
Be still, my soul; your Jesus can repay
from his own fullness all he takes away.

Be still, my soul; the hour is hast'ning on
when we shall be forever with the Lord,
when disappointment, grief, and fear are gone,
sorrow forgot, love's purest joys restored.
Be still my soul; when change and tears are past,
all safe and blessed we shall meet at last.

COMFORTABLE WORDS
Thomas Cranmer

Archbishop Cranmer, coming out of the suffocating legalism of Roman Catholicism, desired to encourage the dear flock who sat in front of him. What would he proclaim on the Lord's Day, especially in preparation for the Lord's Supper?

He is well known for what he told the congregation. He gave them "The Comfortable Words," which were included in the Book of Common Prayer in 1549. These words were Bible verses that focused the hearers on the goodness and graciousness of a forgiving Triune God. Cranmer understood that most of the people in the worship service were used to being told that they could only receive forgiveness through confession to a priest. Cranmer told them that Jesus grants forgiveness, not the Church. And it is to be received by faith alone!

Would these "comfortable words" prepare your heart and mind for participating in the Lord's Supper? Do these words comfort a Christian struggling with assurance? Do they bolster the Christian who is currently experiencing a high level of assurance?

Hear what comfortable words our Savior Christ says to all that truly turn to him.

> *Come to me all that travail, and are heavy laden, and I shall refresh you.*
>
> *God so loved the world, that he gave his only begotten Son to the end that all that believe in him, should not perish, but have everlasting life.*
>
> *Hear also what St. Paul says, "This is a true saying, and worthy of all men to be received, that Jesus Christ came into the world to save sinners."*
>
> *Hear what St. John says, "If any man sin, we have an advocate with the father, Jesus Christ the righteous, and he is the propitiation for our sins."*

Made in the USA
Coppell, TX
21 April 2024

31534628R00111